WANTED

A-Z

THE
WANTED

S A R A H   O L I V E R

JOHN BLAKE

Published by John Blake Publishing Ltd,
3 Bramber Court, 2 Bramber Road,
London W14 9PB, England

www.johnblakepublishing.co.uk

First published in paperback in 2010

ISBN: 978 184358 329 5

British Library Cataloguing-in-Publication Data:

A catalogue record for this book is available from the British Library.

Design by www.envydesign.co.uk

Printed in Great Britain by CPI Bookmarque, Croydon, CR0 4TD

3 5 7 9 10 8 6 4 2

All pictures courtesy of Wenn Images, except pages vi, 8, 13, 16, 27, 28,
37, 52, 78, 125, 138, 150, 156, 174, 198, 204, 220, 224, 243, 244
which are courtesy of Press Association.

Papers used by John Blake Publishing are natural, recyclable products made
from wood grown in sustainable forests. The manufacturing processes
conform to the environmental regulations of the country of origin.

Every attempt has been made to contact the relevant copyright-holders,
but some were unobtainable. We would be grateful
if the appropriate people could contact us.

ACKNOWLEDGEMENTS

Dedicated with love to Mum, Dad, Grandad Harry, Nanna Elsie, Grandad Norman, Nanna Dot, Liz, Dan and Robin.

This book wouldn't have been written without the support of my husband Jon and my editor Joel. Thanks to Christina, Susy and the rest of my friends from the Professional Writing MA at University College Falmouth. A big thank you to Emily, Gail, Victoria, Rachel, Rebecca and Bethany – I love you all so much.

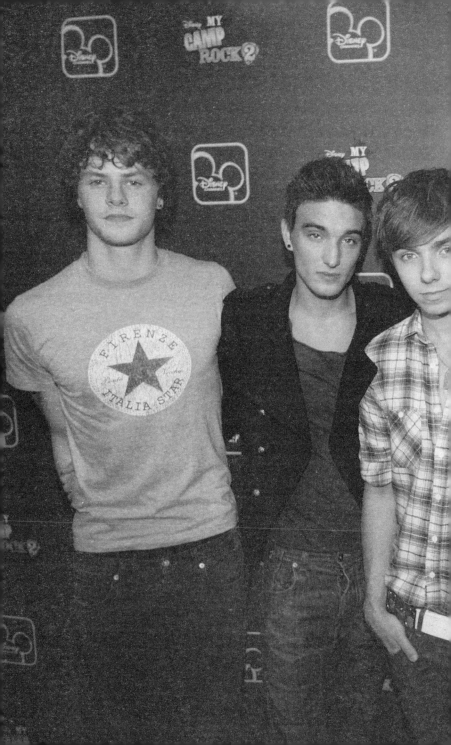

INTRODUCTION

The Wanted A-Z is jam-packed with everything you need to know about the UK's hottest boy band. No other book goes into so much detail or tells all the secrets from the tour van and behind the scenes. Read all about Jay snogging a fan and Britney kissing Nathan. Find out what pranks the boys have pulled on each other and why Tom knows all the words to Take That's biggest hits.

Sarah Oliver is a celebrity journalist who knows more about The Wanted than any other journalist on the planet. She has worked with The Wanted's biggest fans, who have been supporting Jay, Max, Tom, Nathan and Siva since the very beginning. You can follow Sarah on Twitter (http://Twitter.com/SarahOliverAtoZ).

This is the fifth book in the A-Z series. Why not check out *Robert Pattinson A-Z*, *Taylor Lautner A-Z* or *The Completely Unofficial Glee A-Z*? You can read this book from start to finish, or dip in and out of it, as you prefer.

A is for...

Albums

Max, Tom, Siva, Nathan and Jay couldn't wait for fans to listen to their first album. It's a dream for any musician to have their own album but it was extra special for the Wanted boys. They'd worked so hard that they couldn't contain their excitement when it was announced in August 2010 that their first album would be coming out on 25 October – and that there would be a different cover for each member of the band.

Fans were equally as excited and quickly pre-ordered the album the second they were able to. The hard thing for fans was choosing which cover to go for: did they want Siva on the cover, or Jay… or Max? In the end many fans pre-ordered all five versions of the album to show the boys that they loved them all equally. It will be interesting to see whether one day the record company will reveal which album was the most popular and which was the least. In some ways it would be good to see who was the fans' favourite but on the other hand it would make whoever came in last place feel rubbish.

Unlike other pop acts who record their first single, release it and then start work on their album, the boys had already finished their album by the time 'All Time Low' was released for digital download on 25 July 2010. This was a big risk for the record company because it costs a lot of money and takes time to record an album – especially to create one as good as Max, Tom, Siva, Nathan and Jay have done. If 'All Time Low' hadn't done well, and the boys had failed to get a big fanbase, the record company wouldn't have bothered to release the album even though it had already been recorded. They wouldn't have wanted to spend more money promoting it.

Recording their first album wasn't a walk in the park for The Wanted – it was hard work! They had to get to know each other really well before they started and then they had to choose songs they wanted to record, write some of their own and work with big songwriters too. They had to decide what they wanted their sound to be, and what fans would want to hear. This was quite tricky because they didn't have many fans to start with as they hadn't been performing anywhere. They didn't want to create an album with one great song, three good songs and eight average songs. They wanted 12 great songs on the album so ended up recording 25 so they could pick the very best to feature on the album.

Tom told 4Music what they were trying to achieve with their first album. He said, 'We've tried to make the album so that different people can listen to it. Some people will like one track but then other people will like another track. It's got different genres.'

Max is a big fan of the pop tracks on the album but he liked doing the big ballad too. He likes the different rhythms and the way the album appeals to people of all ages. It isn't a stereotypical boy band album either, because they have written some of the tracks and it isn't full of covers. Max, Tom, Siva, Nathan and Jay picked their favourite 11 but it was hard picking the final one. They had three more they wanted to include but the final decision was made by their record company.

Max, Tom, Siva, Nathan and Jay revealed to Orange during an interview: 'On the album we wrote about 60% of the songs; we've got Guy Chambers and Taio Cruz writing on the album too. There's such a mixed bag and for our first album we never expected to be working with such a high level of people.'

Jay talked about how they went about writing their

3

own tracks in another interview with Nokia Music. He said, 'Some days the record label will send us to a studio and say, "Write a song," and it just kind of happens. Some days we just feel like writing a song so someone will start doing something on a guitar, we'll maybe sing over it and see where it goes.'

When it came to naming the album they had so many ideas. They love their track 'Behind Bars' so thought it would make a good name for the album but they knew the final decision would be made by their record company. Most new artists have their first album named after themselves, so they can't have been surprised when they were told there's would be too.

One fan reviewed the album on HMV's site in August, two months before it came out, and gave it 5 stars out of 5 – even though she hadn't heard it. She wrote, 'These guys are going to be BIG!! you should pre-order this CD now because this is going to be sold out as soon as it is released! Their first single 'All Time Low' went straight to number one, and I am sure this album will too! They are all different people with different styles so there will be a song for everybody! Can't wait for it to be released.'

Siva, Max, Tom, Jay and Nathan don't want their first album to be their last so really need their fans to buy as many copies of the album as possible. It was a clever move by their record company to have a cover for each of the boys – because it will maximise sales. On their official website super fan Millie Thorne wrote, 'I'm going to get all five :) Much love' and huge Tom fan Selina wrote, 'I'm so gonna get all five and one with everyone on it and an extra Tom one because he is the hottest.'

Hopefully they will be releasing a new album every year from now on, and going on a tour every year too. It will be hard to make their second album better than their first but the boys are up for the challenge!

'All Time Low'

The Wanted's first single was called 'All Time Low' and it was a huge hit as soon as it was released. It was available for download on 25 July 2010 and a CD version was available in shops the day after. It charted at number 1 in the UK and number 19 in Ireland. The CD version proved to be so popular that HMV sold out of copies, but thankfully it didn't take them long to restock. The Wanted did signings in several cities and towns, and hundreds of fans queued for hours just to catch a glimpse of them at each location.

The first question that the band got asked in interviews whilst they were promoting the single was 'What is it about?' A lot of the time Jay was the person nominated to answer and he soon explained the song's main theme and who wrote the track. Jay said in one

NATHAN AND SIVA PERFORM 'ALL TIME LOW'.

interview with First TV, 'It was written by Ed Drewett, the guy who features on Professor Green's "I Need You Tonight," and Steve Mac and it's about when a girl's in your head and she's ruining your day and you just can't get up from it.'

'All Time Low' writers

Ed Drewett

Ed is one of the best songwriters around even though he's only in his early twenties. He's from

Harlow in Essex and sings as well as writing songs. He is signed to EMI Virgin Records. Ed Drewett kind of knows how the boys felt when they were recognised for the first time – because he was in the final 20 contestants on the Andrew Lloyd Webber show *Any Dream Will Do* back in 2007. He was recognised in the street back then but is recognised less now. Ed is best known for a single he did with Professor Green called 'I Need You Tonight'. It didn't do as well as 'All Time Low' though – it only got to number three in the chart. As well as writing for The Wanted and other stars, Ed has been working on his own music. His fans were thrilled when they found out he'd be releasing his first album in early 2011. They think his track 'Champagne Lemonade' is great and hope it gets lots of airplay on the radio.

Steve Mac
Steven Mac knows talent when he sees it as he's produced over 20 number 1 singles in the UK, loads of hit albums… and owns Rokstone Studios in London. He's written and produced songs for JLS, Susan Boyle, Westlife, Leona Lewis, Kelly Clarkson… and loads more of the world's top artists.

Steve has received three BMI USA Writers

awards, was named MMF Producer Of The Year in 2002 and three of his songs have won Record Of The Year. In 2009 he was nominated for Producer of the Year at the Music Producers Guild Awards and in 2010 he won the 'Best Single' Brit Award for the JLS song, 'Beat Again'. The Wanted were so privileged to get to work with him so early in their careers. He has so much talent and is great at picking and writing songs that will be huge hits.

Wayne Hector

Wayne Hector is one of the UK's most successful songwriters of all time. He is signed to Sony ATV Music Publishing and has written songs for Britney Spears, Carrie Underwood, Westlife, Charlotte Church and the Pussycat Dolls just to name a few. He was the man behind Westlife's 'Swear It Again' and 'Flying Without Wings'. Like Steve Mac, he has also written for JLS. All three men worked together to create 'All Time Low', the perfect debut single for The Wanted.

You would think that with 'All Time Low' being such a great track, radio stations would have been queuing up to play it as soon as they were able to. Many were, but not Radio 1. For some reason Radio 1 refused to air it, which left thousands of The Wanted's fans feeling angry and frustrated. They weren't the only ones, as the band were disappointed too. They knew that 'All Time Low' had to perform well, otherwise they would be dropped by their record label. So many boy bands and girl bands get dropped once their debut single fails to make the top 40. Instead of feeling defeated, Max, Tom, Siva, Nathan and Jay remained confident that 'All Time Low' was going to be a hit so explored other avenues. They did a schools tour, performed in clubs, performed in shopping centres – anything to promote the single. They visited so many radio stations and TV stations up and down the UK, not stopping for a moment. They needed to create a buzz around themselves and their single.

Even though Radio 1 wouldn't play 'All Time Low', JLS managed to get it on there as they were temporarily given control of Radio 1 playlists during the DJ slot on the 519 show. JLS wanted to show everyone how much they like The Wanted and 'All Time Low'. Max and the rest of the boys were very grateful and will no doubt return the favour one day.

It wasn't just radio stations who were crazy about the single – as soon as the general public heard it they started tapping their feet and singing along. It was so catchy and straight away the band had girls declaring their love for them and saying that they were the best band ever.

Fan Sarah from Manchester gave the single 5 stars out of 5 in her review on HMV's site. She wrote: 'I bought mine 9am Monday morning (day of release)! The single sold out within the space of 5 minutes. Then got my poster signed by all the boys, best day ever, the single is amazing, so is the fight for this love cover. Best new boy band… these guys will be big, watch this space!'

Even the critics who enjoy slating new releases gave it the thumbs up. Ryan Love from Digital Spy awarded the single 4 stars out of 5 in his review. He wrote: 'Even though The Wanted clearly fulfil the boy band archetype – five good-looking guys who can hold a few notes together – this debut single is actually a bit of a surprise. The opening strings are quite simply immense… the lyrics slightly less so. "When I'm standing on the yellow line/Waiting at the station/Or I'm late for work/A vital presentation" has to be heard several times to be believed. However, even a howler like that can't spoil this fresh 'n' fizzy indie-tinged pop gem. It's too soon to tell whether The Wanted will have JLS cranking up their ab sets in fear, but for now they can celebrate the fact that one of them has just stolen Sophie Ellis-Bextor's Best Cheekbones In Pop crown. Nice work, Siva!'

Fraser McAlpine from Radio 1 said in his review: 'We're not dealing with a bunch of kids here, this is a more mature form of boy band. A nearly-man band,

NATHAN SAYS HELLO TO FANS DURING A PERFORMANCE OF 'ALL TIME LOW'.

if you like… This is good. And even if the best bit shamelessly pinches its melody from Coldplay's "The Scientist" – a song which seems to have been responsible for 56% of all melody in the noughties – it does at least do it while boasting a memorable line, with a devilish internal rhyme which more than makes up for it: "I'm in pieces, seems like peace is the only thing I'll never know." See what I mean? That's classy.'

Bill Lamb from About.com said: 'Is there room for another new boy band to storm the charts? The new English/Irish boy band The Wanted say unequivocally yes, and, based on the strength of this debut single "All Time Low" it is difficult to argue with them.' He praised the 'Opening string figure, solid, accented vocals and lyrics with emotional resonance.'

'All Time Low' isn't a predictable boy band song. Even the band have difficulty defining it. Tom thinks it's got an indie-pop vibe but Tom doesn't think it's indie at all. Max told 4Music he thinks it's 'dead-good pop'. Nathan thinks it's anthemic.

SHOOTING THE VIDEO

Everyone knows that at some point every boy band shoots a video in a derelict warehouse so The Wanted boys thought they'd get their warehouse video out of the way first. Max joked to one interviewer that it looked like their shared house – full of rubbish and looking a state.

In the video Tom wears some grey trousers that are actually Max's favourite trousers. He was a bit miffed that Tom stole his style because once people saw the video he thought they would think that he was wearing Tom's trousers in interviews, even though he had them first. He didn't want to stop wearing them but he didn't want people saying 'Max has stolen Tom's trousers' either. When Siva sits on the edge in the video, high above Nathan who is dancing, he is wearing a safety harness, just in case he fell off. No one wanted to risk Siva seriously injuring himself.

Also whilst they were filming the part where Jay dances on some rubble he ended up falling over in front of a lot of people. A few members of the group kept asking for some beers as they were waiting around to shoot their scenes but they kept being told no – alcohol wasn't allowed on set. In total the boys had to stay up for over 24 hours to film the video even though it is only 3 minutes and 27 seconds long. They must have been shattered by the time they got to crawl into their beds – they'd been up since before 5am.

PROMOTING THE SINGLE

The boys were so excited when copies of the single were delivered to their house. They rushed to the door

to collect the two boxes. When they opened the first box they discovered some 'The Wanted' branded pens. They were nice but they wanted to see the singles more so quickly opened the second box. Tom took a CD and sprinted into the lounge to put it on. The boys love 'All Time Low'! Take a look at their Regional Radio Tour Schedule, and you can see how busy the boys were just during one week leading up to the single coming out (and how many miles they had to travel). Wednesday in particular was a long day on the road and they had to do seven interviews too. It's not surprising that they didn't get much sleep that week!

Monday 28 June
09.30–10.00 Oxford FM (Oxford) – Live Breakfast interview
11.30–12.00 Star Radio (Bristol)
14.00–14.30 The Wave (Swansea)
16.30–17.00 Red Dragon (Cardiff)
Tuesday 29 June
10.00–10.30 BRBM (Birmingham)
10.30–11.00 Galaxy (Birmingham)
12.30–13.30 Trent FM (Nottingham)
14.30–15.00 Lincs FM (Lincoln)
16.30–17.00 Hallam FM (Sheffield)
Wednesday 30 June
09.30–10.00 Viking FM (Hull)

11.00–11.30 Radio Aire (Leeds)
11.45–12.15 Galaxy (Leeds)
14.00–14.30 The Pulse (Bradford)
15.30–16.30 In Demand (Manchester)
17.00–17.30 Real Radio (Manchester)
18.30–19.00 Silk FM (Macclesfield)
Thursday 1 July
10.30–11.00 Radio City (Liverpool)
12.00–12.30 Wish FM (Wigan)
13.00–13.30 Rock FM (Preston)
Friday 2 July
11.00–11.30 Forth One (Edinburgh)
12.30–13.00 Real Radio Scotland (Glasgow)
13.30–14.00 Galaxy Scotland (Glasgow)
14.30–15.30 Clyde Radio (Glasgow)

They were even busier the week it came out. When they went to Nottingham to do a signing in HMV the store sold all 600 copies of the single. Girls queued right around the block for a chance to see them and one girl even flew in from Canada for the opportunity. Jay loved the love they got in his home town and pinched a cardboard sign from the HMV signing for his bedroom wall.

In the week of the release they were so busy that sometimes they didn't know whether they were doing a performance or a signing until they walked into the room filled with screaming fans and their manager Jayne told them. It's surprising that they had any voices left by the end of the week. Some fans gave them little gifts when they got to the front of the signing queue. Nathan was very grateful for the doughnuts he was given to share with the rest of the group – signing hundreds of autographs makes Nathan hungry!

CELEBRATING

The boys actually started celebrating the success of the single days before the official chart was announced on Sunday 1 August, because they were so pleased to be in the Top 20. They had some idea that they might chart at number one because they had been leading in the midweek sales but they didn't want to get too over-excited in case it didn't happen.

Nathan explained to *This Is Gloucestershire*: 'At the start of the week I heard that we were in the top 20 and I ran down the stairs to tell the boys. We were watching the screen and we just kept climbing. We hoped to be in the top 40, actually we were praying to be in the top 40, so to get a number one was just mental. The boys, the management and everyone have been great and we have done so much better than we expected.'

The boys were in the Radio 1 studios on the Sunday when they got the news they were number 1, which

was strange considering Radio 1 had been refusing to play 'All Time Low' for weeks. It is the biggest chart show so it made sense that they were there rather than at a smaller station. Radio 1 listeners could hear what was going on and there was a webcam so people could visit the Radio 1 site to watch what was happening in the studio live. The boys held up pieces of paper with the chart numbers on whilst Reggie Yates read out the Top Ten. They all did silly dancing, Siva started them off but Jay was the funniest because he mimed the songs and it looked on the webcam like he was really singing. Each time Reggie read out a number the boys didn't know if it was going to be them but by the time Nathan was stood with only the 'Number One' piece of paper in his hand they knew they had done it. They told Reggie how happy they were and how grateful they were before Max did a shout out to his dad, nan and grandad who were having a party. Jay asked to do a shout out to their management who picked them and 'turned their lives right around.' Their manager Jayne was stood right next to Siva and shed a tear. She loves the boys so much and was so touched that they thanked her.

As well as fans of The Wanted logging on to the website to watch them live, the families of Max, Tom, Siva, Nathan and Jay did as well. Max's family weren't the only ones to throw a party. Tom's family held a party in their house so they could celebrate together with their friends and extended family. Tom's dad Nigel cracked open the champagne to toast his son and the other boys. It was just a shame Tom couldn't be there – but he still had a great night. The boys headed out to Whisky Mist which is a trendy club in Mayfair. It's popular with royals, footballers and pop stars. It is an exclusive club so you have to be a member to get in. They had a party and lots of famous faces helped them celebrate – including the lovely Leona Lewis. Newspapers reported the next day that Leona and Max got chatting at the bar and swapped mobile numbers but no official statement has been released. The boys sipped champagne with mini fireworks and things got a bit messy. Tom ended up getting his grey vest stained but he didn't let it ruin his night.

They ended up spending the month celebrating because they were so happy to be at number one. They didn't want the party to end.

Jay loves 'All Time Low' and how it has changed his life so much that he is thinking about getting a constant reminder of the single. He confided to the *Daily Star*, 'I'm thinking about getting a tattoo with the name of the first single drawn in. I'm not going to regret it, we'll be around a long time.'

Max is equally as passionate about the band and told a journalist from Crave on Music at Leeds Party in the

Park before the track charted, 'If we get to number one, I'll get "The Wanted" tattooed on me bum.'

Siva didn't want an 'All Time Low' tattoo to remember the single, so instead he went guitar shopping and picked up a very special guitar that he will treasure forever.

Lots of bands attempt to have a number one single but never manage to achieve it. They might have a great song but only manage to get it to number two or number three. The Wanted managed to get to number one with their first attempt. Celebritain.com asked Max how they got it so right. He replied, 'I haven't got a clue. I don't know. We've worked really hard but we just get up in the morning and go and do it. We don't think to ourselves that we should be at number one. I can't get my head around it really. Lori and Jayne are on it everyday, we take videos all the time and they have to get it all down so they slave away on it all the time.'

Even though the band has sung 'All Time Low' hundreds of times they still love performing it and enjoy listening to it when it comes on the radio. They were very excited when it was played in a club for the first time.

Jay tweeted on 15 August 2010: 'We're in blackpool, and for the 1st time we was in a club that played us - buzzin!!!!!! No one danced, guttin, shrug, we did! X What a good night! Literally every1 we met was welllll

SIVA TALKS TO A FAN DURING THE PROMOTION OF THE WANTED'S DEBUT SINGLE

sound – that group in the burger place in the mornin if you read this you was belters!'

Imagine being in a burger bar in the early hours and seeing The Wanted walk in and order some food, you'd think you were dreaming!

The Next Step

Before the single came out in the UK the boys knew that their record company would want them to promote it in other countries if it was successful. They knew that Germany would be the first country but that they could end up doing a European tour if people outside the UK liked their music enough.

On the 16th August Tom tweeted RT @thewantedmusic: 'Calling all TW fans based in GERMANY! Tweet us now & include #TWGermany in your reply. Can't wait to go.never been to germany x'

Auditions

The boys had to audition to get in the band. Siva got a phone call telling him about the auditions, Nathan was told about them by the Sylvia Young Agency and the others answered an ad in *The Stage* newspaper. *The Stage* has been used to put together some great bands over the years including the Spice Girls. The ad was placed by Jayne Collins who was set to manage the band.

There were lots of people who wanted to be in the band so Jayne held mass auditions. The first round of auditions took place in February 2009. She saw so many talented boys during the nine months it took to find the final five members of the band. She picked Tom, Nathan and Jay first and they only had to do two rounds of auditions. She knew virtually straight away

that they would be perfect for the band, and she was bowled over by Jay's voice. She picked Siva and Max during the second sweep of auditions as she thought they would complement Tom, Nathan and Jay. The official announcement of who was in the band was

AUDITIONS FOR THE BAND BEGAN IN FEBRUARY 2009.

made in the Autumn. Many people think the band only got to know each other when they were brought together but this wasn't the case at all. Throughout the audition process they'd seen each other, Siva knew Jay first because they were in the same harmony group during some of the auditions.

The boys aren't ashamed of being manufactured. They fully appreciate the work Jayne and her team have put in to nurturing them and making them the best band they can be. They are five very different guys but they all get on really well. Siva revealed to 4Music, 'I think if there were too similar personalities, it just wouldn't work as we'd compete.' Tom added, 'There's something for everyone.'

Awards

The boys presented their first ever award at the Arqiva Commercial Radio Awards on 17 June 2010. While he was getting ready Jay admitted that he'd won an award in the past, for being 'The Best Runner-up' during a week's holiday at Butlins. There had been lots of competitions and races throughout the week but Jay had been beaten every time. That's why they decided to give him an award. Nathan is the member of the band who has won the most awards and competitions even though he is the youngest. His awards have been for

THE BOYS AND A VERY SPECIAL GUEST POSE FOR A PHOTO.

singing and performing.

Jay will be winning lots more awards now he is in the band. The Wanted have so much talent that they are going to end up needing lots of trophy cabinets to display all their trophies in the next year or two. They are unique and their songs are so good that they'll be winning Brit Awards, MTV Europe Music Awards, Music Video Awards and Nickelodeon Kids' Choice Awards in no time at all.

B is for...

Birthdays

For Jay's 20th birthday he couldn't go home to spend the day with his family so the band made sure he had a great day. They got him a birthday cake and Max gave him a kiss on the cheek to 'welcome him into adulthood'.

When they arrived at Radio 1 for an interview there were loads of fans there and they all sang 'Happy Birthday'. Jay got so many presents, cards, cakes and balloons that he struggled to carry them into the building. The fans spoiled him rotten all day but they gave the other members small presents so they wouldn't feel left out. Siva was given a pint of milk and some Oreos. Max got an amazing Elvis memento book that had CDs, copies of newspaper articles and loads of interesting Elvis things in it. It was the best present Max had ever been given by a fan – and it wasn't even his birthday!

One of Jay's most treasured possessions is a framed poster of *Avatar* with film cells around the edge, which he was given for his birthday. One fan sent him a Starbucks card so he went for a drinks run. That was a very well thought out present. His favourite birthday card was a personalised Moonpig-style one that looked like a newspaper. The opening line was 'Breaking News! Jay McGuiness joins the Na'Vi!' and it had a picture of him with a blue face (from *Avatar*). It was sent by Lauren Hembrough and her friend.

Boy bands

The Wanted are a boy band and they're not ashamed to admit it. There has been a stigma about boy bands for quite a few years but even more so for manufactured boy bands. JLS had an easy ride because they had put themselves together and appeared on *The X Factor*. Radio 1 DJ Jo Whiley told journalist Dean Piper when they were discussing The Wanted: 'It's just very calculated stuff – pulling together a few hot lads. It's not anything new.'

Jay sees being labelled as a boy band as a great thing

JAY GIVES HIS
AVATAR FILM
POSTER THE
THUMBS-UP!

and he wants to see more boy bands in the charts. In many ways Jay is right, there hasn't been a decent boy band (apart from JLS) since Blue, and they split up in 2005. Really there is no other word that the media could use to describe The Wanted because they are a boy band. Max explained to 4Music why he thinks boy band has become 'an illegal term.' He said: 'I think it just got to the point where boy bands were totally uncool. If you even admitted to half-liking one, then you became uncool.'

The boys have excellent singing voices and look gorgeous but interviewers still want to know what makes them unique. The Wanted always say it's Siva, because he is an Asian Dubliner and no other boy band has had one of them!

Getting in the group was a big deal for Jay and he decided to do his homework. He revealed to the *Metro*: 'I was a total geek when I got in this group and decided to thoroughly research boy bands. I haven't seen one we're similar to. Westlife just stand there and sing; we jump around like idiots. We have dance routines but we're not as good as *N Sync. I think we're a new species of band. Although I might be flattering myself.'

If the boys had to say what was the best thing about being in a boy band, Max and Tom would say the girls because they love the attention they receive from hot girls. Nathan would say being on stage and performing because that is what he has always wanted to do since

NATHAN, JAY, MAX, TOM, AND SIVA POSE FOR A PICTURE PRIOR TO GOING ON *THIS MORNING*.

he was six years old. The rest of the group think that Nathan is the laziest member of The Wanted but he says he isn't. Jay loves being on stage but also loves the female attention he gets from being in the band – so he can't decide. Skittles lover Siva says he loves it when he gets sent Skittles from fans the most but he must be joking because there must be dozens of better things about being in The Wanted than that.

If they had to pick one word to describe themselves Tom would pick cheeky, Nathan would pick cute, Jay would pick geeky, Max would pick sexy and Siva would pick Zen. Siva says Zen means being the calmest one. Even though Max picked the word sexy they all could have, because they are all pretty sexy!

The boys aren't just good looking singers; they can play musical instruments too. Jay told Nokia Music, 'Siva and Tom are really musical. They both play guitar and Nathan plays piano. We really do care about the music side of it and want to make good tunes that we'd actually listen to. Obviously you can't say that other boy bands don't, but from my experience they sound a bit… not created, but churned out a bit.'

Bullying

When the boys go to clubs Nathan gets picked on by jealous lads. They don't like the way girls pay the band

SIVA IS SAID TO BE ONE OF
THE MOST MUSICAL MEMBERS
OF THE WANTED.

loads of attention. They want the girls to fancy them so decide to take it out on Nathan, because he's the youngest. Jay, Max, Siva and Tom notice when this happens and stick up for Nathan. They won't let anyone bully their mate. They don't mind teasing him themselves but they're just having a laugh, they don't mean anything by it.

There has been the odd time when the band have accidentally upset a fan and the fan gets the impression that they are picking on them. One day they were talking to a fan and one of the band members was missing. Someone said they were a man down so Jay said to the fan 'You can be the extra man.' The girl was really upset and thought that Jay was saying she looked like a man. He wasn't saying it to be mean, he was just saying she could be in the band. If he'd said the same thing to 100 girls, 99 of them would have taken it how he meant it, and only one would take it the wrong way… it just so happened that he spoke to the wrong girl!

Another time Jay got in a fan's bad books was when Max was having a photo taken with a fan. Jay admitted to *Teen Today* that he did the peace sign behind her head for fun and she flipped. She told Jay that she hated him. She probably didn't mean it but sometimes the band forget that for fans getting the opportunity to meet them can be a once in a lifetime thing, and they want it to be perfect.

THE WANTED MEET THEIR ADORING FANS.

The media seem to enjoy having digs at The Wanted whenever they can but Max, Tom, Siva, Nathan and Jay don't let it get to them. They refuse to be bullied. No one likes reading negative things in the press about themselves but when the press attack a member of their families it really hurts.

In the future it would be great if the band could become spokespeople for a bullying charity because they know what it's like to be bullied and they are great role models. They would be able to teach children that you should never listen to bullies when they say you can't do something or be something you want to be. A few years ago when they told people they wanted to be in a boy band some people would have laughed and said it would never happen – they proved them wrong. The whole band would be able to inspire children to dream big dreams.

C is for...

Charity Work

Being famous has allowed Max, Tom, Siva, Nathan and Jay to help raise a lot of money for charity. All the boys are passionate about charity work and are always willing to step in and do what they can to help.

In June 2010 The Wanted performed at Cash for Kids Night at Hamilton Park to raise money for needy children in the local area. The boys were one of the warm-up acts before The Saturdays took to the stage. Back then, they didn't have a single to push so no one could say they did it to promote their single. They actually did it because they wanted to do something for a worthy charity. The Wanted are just five honest lads who enjoy spending their free time helping others.

In August 2010 the boys volunteered to head up to Scotland to take part in a charity car boot sale. The event was backed by Real Radio and *The Scottish Sun* and its aim was to raise as much money as possible for the Children's Hospice Association of Scotland. Lots of celebs donated things to be sold at the car boot but The Wanted wanted to be there in person. They performed alongside Alesha Dixon and donated lots of signed merchandise.

They loved performing at the Heroes Concert at Twickenham Stadium on 12 September 2010. The concert was held to raise money for Help For Heroes which is a charity that helps support injured soldiers, ex-soldiers and their families. The boys said when it was announced they were in the line-up, 'It's an absolute pleasure for us to be taking part in this show. Our servicemen and women do a superb job and if we can help in any way then that's what we'll do. Help for Heroes is a cracking charity and we're so honoured to be asked to perform.'

Crushes

The Wanted are the hottest boy band around so it's no surprise that thousands of girls have crushes on them.

MAX AND TOM HAVE A CHAT BEFORE SAYING 'HI' TO THEIR FANS.

It's not just girls in the UK or Ireland either – girls in Germany, America, Canada and… well, everywhere have the hots for Jay, Siva, Max, Tom and Nathan.

The band think that Max is the heartthrob of The Wanted but that Tom would like to think that he is. Siva jokes that when they are in a club he just points at Max and tells girls, 'Here he is.' He says Max gets swamped all the time. Do you think Max is the hottest? Or does another member of The Wanted get your vote?

Max told one interviewer, 'The fans are already forming teams and I'm racing ahead, honestly! Maybe it's the shaved head and manly chest, I dunno. But the other lads hate it!'

Max and the rest of the boys might think that more girls have crushes on him more than any other member of the band but during their school concerts it was quite often Nathan that the girls fancied. With all five boys being very different virtually every girl can find her ideal crush in the band. If you like lads with model looks you might fancy Siva but if you prefer your lads cheeky you might prefer Tom (they don't get much cheekier than Tom!). He says that if he was a girl and had to pick a member of The Wanted to date he would pick all of them!

During one interview the band were asked to stand in a line according to who flirts the most. Tom was at the top, followed by Max. Initially Jay was third but he swapped places with Nathan because he thinks that Nathan flirts more with fans. Siva was in last place and is the least flirty member of The Wanted because he has a girlfriend.

When the band gets interviewed sometimes the journalists or presenters can't help but find themselves developing a bit of a crush. T4 presenter Miquita Oliver admitted after her first interview with the boys that if she had to pick it one member of The Wanted to date it would be Jay. She thinks he's cute and he's closer to her in age than Nathan, who is the baby of the band.

The Wanted have their own crushes on celebrities so know what it's like to have a crush on someone you think is out of your league (even though they might not be.) Jay has a thing for Hayley Williams who is the lead singer of the American rock band Paramore. He confessed to the *Metro*: 'She's a cracker. She's beautiful. I've only seen her on TV but she's got the perfect mouth. She's hot.'

If Jay met Hayley in real life he might have a problem getting her to like him as much as he likes her. He told *Bliss*: I'm a goofball and I'll often say something silly to a hot girl, and they'll just look at me all disgusted!'

The press have said in the past that Max is dating

JAY IS *T4* PRESENTER MIQUITA OLIVER'S FAVOURITE MEMBER OF THE WANTED.

Vanessa from The Saturdays because they got close when they were on tour together. This wasn't true and Max has admitted that Mollie is his favourite even though she has been dating her boyfriend Andy Brown for well over a year. Andy was one of Max's bandmates in Avenue. This just shows how small the showbiz world is. Jay is actually the band member who finds Vanessa the most attractive!

Siva doesn't have crushes on the famous girls they meet on nights out, at celebrity parties or concerts. When he met Una from The Saturdays he said, 'Is it me, or am I really tall?' according to Jay on a Wanted Wednesday video. Jay couldn't believe that Siva said that when he could have said a million other things. Tom has a bit of a crush on her though and he's dated her (in his dreams).

Max likes The Saturdays too but Cheryl Tweedy is his number one celebrity crush. He thinks she's gorgeous. He also has a bit of a soft spot for Pixie Lott. It must be weird fancying The Saturdays and Pixie Lott because they are friends of the band and hang out together.

In real life Nathan says he likes quiet girls but the celebrity he would most like to kiss is Miley Cyrus (who is the opposite of quiet). Miley says she can't stop talking and it seems strange that Nathan would pick her as his celebrity crush. Maybe he likes her because she's

NATHAN HAS A CRUSH ON GIRLS ALOUD STAR, CHERYL TWEEDY.

nearer his age than other celebrity women. Other women that Nathan has a bit of a crush on are Abbey Clancy, Megan Fox and Cheryl Tweedy.

D is for...

Dreams

Being in the band has made Tom, Jay, Max, Nathan and Siva dream big dreams. Their manager Jayne and the rest of the people behind the scenes know they have great potential and can achieve anything they put their minds to.

Max dreams about being at the Brits and having a table there. He doesn't admit to wanting to perform on the Brits stage but most fans know he would jump at the chance. Every big artist wants to perform during the awards show and show the best of the music industry what they are made of.

Siva hasn't really had the chance to dream about

what he wants The Wanted to achieve in the future. He's just enjoying every moment of what's happening now. All the boys are looking forward to having their own tour but they know they will be even busier then. They will have to put in so much time and energy into creating the best show for their fans and it will be so tiring performing a two-hour show every night. It will be even harder for Siva to see his girlfriend because they will be touring all over the place.

Tom likes to think that the band will go to America one day so that is his big dream. Not many UK artists manage to break America so it would be a great achievement for The Wanted if they got one of their songs in the US Top 20. Tom has never had a problem dreaming big dreams because he's always been ambitious and hard-working.

The Wanted might have some great tracks on their first album but they would love to record some duets for their second album. They would love to sing alongside some music legends. The whole band would love it if Stevie Wonder would record something with them but they don't think he'd be up for it. Nathan thinks it would be cool to record something with Dizzee Rascal and Siva would like to perform with Justin Bieber one day.

E is for...

Example

Example is a UK rapper and singer. His full name is Elliot John Gleave. He annoyed The Wanted and their fans back in July 2010 when he said that the band look like 'extras from *Hollyoaks*'.

Example was being interviewed by The Razz at Glasgow's In:Demand Live when he was asked what he thought of 'All Time Low'. He said it was catchy but added: 'They are just so perfect looking, all of them. It's like some guy has spotted them loitering on set and said, "You wanna be in a band?"'

The Wanted found out what he said and got their own back by saying that Example looks like Marlon

UK RAP-STAR AND SINGER, EXAMPLE.

from *Emmerdale*. Siva jokingly confided in the Scottish *Daily Record*: 'I'm upset that he just thinks we look like extras, not even main actors.' Nathan didn't see Example's comment about them looking like *Hollyoaks* extras as a bad thing because *Hollyoaks* people are good-looking.

A few days later Siva spotted Example on the tube and decided to say hello. He didn't want to just ignore him and pretend he hadn't noticed the rapper. Example tweeted: 'He comes over and says, "Hi mate I'm Siva, love your single, didn't recognise you with your hair down."'

It sounds like Example and The Wanted have decided to forget what was said and they are all going to move on. If they bump into each other again they will probably just say hello and shake hands. Siva, Jay, Max, Nathan and Tom aren't the type of people to hold grudges.

Exercise

You don't get to look as toned as Tom and Max do without exercising. Nathan might hate it, but if he wants to look as toned as Tom and Max then he is going to have to find time to exercise a bit more. If he doesn't want to, though, his fans won't mind – they love him just the way he is.

HUNKY TOM SIGNS
A POSTER

Siva is really into exercising and likes doing press-ups in the morning – he can do over 200 in one go. Nathan is the opposite – he has never done 200 sit-ups in his life. Max has some big weights in his room for when he fancies exercising. They don't have the time to nip to a gym for a workout. People might think exercising wouldn't be a priority for lads in a boy band but it is. They have to be able to move around a stage without getting out of breath, and be able to keep performing for hours at a time as they often have to go from one place to the next during a day. Being in a boy band isn't a 9 to 5 job. In many ways The Wanted have it harder than other music artists because they don't stand in one place when they perform and they don't like sitting on stools either!

The boys are so busy all the time that they have to exercise when and where they can. Sometimes getting up half an hour before the other boys can be the best thing to do, other times they just find 10 minutes to do some exercise as they are out and about.

When they went to do an interview with Radio 2, Siva, Nathan, Tom and Jay went in the lift because the studio was on the sixth floor. Max decided that he needed the exercise so took the stairs – he regretted it afterwards as each floor had three sets of stairs so in total he had to go up 18 flights of stairs. He was shattered and admitted in the interview, 'my thighs were burning!'

F is for...

Fame

Lots of people dream of being famous but few people realise how much hard work is involved. Becoming famous is in many ways easier than staying famous.

Jay talked to his local paper, the *Nottingham Post*, about what it has been like going from auditioning to be in bands to being in The Wanted. He said, 'You would go somewhere, and there would be a crowd of kids screaming because they'd seen us on a YouTube video, and then you would go back to reality. The bubble bursts, and you have to work really hard but now it's all coming together.'

Many people think that The Wanted came out of

LIPSY
LONDON

NTRODUCING TH̶E̶ ̶N̶EW FRAGR

Dream

next →

nex

nowhere to get to number one with 'All Time Low' but that couldn't be further than the truth. They spent so many months building their fanbase and getting people to know who they were and what they were about. At the moment it is mainly young girls who know who they are so they haven't reached the peak of their fame yet. One day everyone will know who they are, and they will be a famous UK boy band known all over Europe and (hopefully) the world.

Jay and the rest of the boys find it weird that they can go to the big TV and Radio stations and see a hundred girls screaming their names but they can nip down to their local shop and won't get recognised. It's pretty cool having the best of both worlds at the moment but soon they will get recognised by everyone and they will have paparazzi following their every move.

Fan mail

If you are a big fan of The Wanted then you might want to get in touch with the band. They are constantly on the move so it's hard to track them down on a day-to-day basis. If you want to tell them how great they are, ask for a signed photo or want to send them something you've made or bought for them then this is the address you need:

The Wanted
MAM
18 Exeter Street
London
WC2E 7DU

You can send the boys anything you want. They love receiving cards and drawings from fans because they really appreciate the time and effort that has gone into making them. They put their favourite pieces of fan mail in their bedrooms and all around their house so they can look at them again and again. If you would like The Wanted to reply to your letter then please include a self-addressed envelope. It can take a while to get a reply because they are so busy but please be patient. They try to reply to as many people as possible but if you don't hear anything back, why not write them another letter? They often use Twitter and YouTube to thank fans for things they have received through the post.

In their house they have a shelf dedicated to the teddy bears they get sent from their fans and another shelf for skittles. They get sent so many that soon they might have to have a whole bookcase for teddies and another one for skittles. The skittles shelf does get emptier though because the band are forever munching on them!

Fans

The Wanted think that their fans are the best fans in the whole wide world. They think that they are so dedicated and the band knows that without their fans' support they would be nothing.

Their fans enjoy meeting other fans as well as the band when they go to signings or to performances. So many good friendships have been formed through these band events and on The Wanted's official forum. Super fan Jessica Sproate reveals, 'There is not one other fan of the Wanted that I have met that I haven't got on with and it's really nice to all be able to be such good support for The Wanted! No matter how many times you meet The Wanted, you're always bound to have fun when you go! The boys love joking around and giving out kisses and cuddles to everyone.'

Siva, Nathan, Max, Jay and Tom are amazed at how accurately their fans can draw them when they are given drawings by fans either in person or through their fan mail address. They really cherish the drawings that have taken fans many hours to draw. They think their fans are super talented!

The boys also love signing autographs but they have to sign so quickly sometimes that Max says his initials start off right but they soon end up looking like different letters. Tom isn't very good at signing

SIVA MEETS A YOUNG
FAN PRIOR TO A LIVE
PERFORMANCE.

his signature so it never looks the same. They will get better though, with practice. Sometimes they will spend three hours solid signing autographs because they don't want to let any fan go home empty-handed. When they're travelling from gig to gig they will often spend the time signing posters and photos to hand out later. Sometimes they will write a special message on the odd one and ask for the fan that gets it to get in touch.

The boys are always surprised how many people turn up to their performances. When they were promoting 'All Time Low' they told Newsbeat, 'We did a gig in Andover, hundreds and hundreds of girls. Nottingham and Birmingham were also crazy.'

In July 2010 it was reported that The Wanted had rescued some fans who were stranded far from home. It was 1am and the boys had just left Manchester's Old Trafford cricket ground when they spotted the fans. They must have been tired after performing but they knew they had to stop. They found out that the fans didn't have enough money for a taxi so Max's dad gave them money out of his own pocket to make sure that they got home okay. The fans must have been so happy to have had the opportunity to talk to Jay, Siva, Max, Nathan and Tom in person.

Most of The Wanted's fans are young girls but some of their tracks will appeal to different types of people.

When Popjustice asked Max who was going to buy their music, he replied, 'I'd say the younger sort, 12 to 18. That would be the predominant age. But I think we might appeal to an older... well we've got one song with an Ennio Morricone sample in it from "The Good, The Bad And The Ugly", and all the mums and dads and older brothers and that say that it's their favourite.'

The boys love all their fans but they have some whom they love more. They are really close to the fans who have been supporting them since the beginning and they know them all by name. When fans are invited to write in with questions they want the boys to answer, the boys often recognise the fan's name and say things like, 'She's really nice' or 'She always asks good questions.'

When BBC Switch asked the boys whether they preferred shy or crazy fans, Nathan said shy, Max and Tom said crazy and Jay and Siva said they liked shy, clean fans. They seem to think that cleanliness is very important!

The boys love the attention they get at gigs and they told *OK!* magazine all about it. Tom said, 'We did a gig at a school the other day and it was mental! When we first did schools, nobody knew us, we'd had no radio play or TV appearances, so it was a bit awkward. But the other day was brilliant, they stormed the stage! Max added, 'I had my bum pinched

THE WANTED BOYS ARE FOLLOWED ALL OVER THE PLACE BY THE PAPARAZZI.
HERE'S NATHAN GREETING A PHOTOGRAPHER WITH A 'THUMBS-UP'!

about 10 times – one of them had a right grab and clung onto it for ages!'

Fans do love pinching the lads' bums whenever they can. They just reach out and grab them as the band goes past. Jay, Nathan, Max, Tom and Siva must have sore bums some days as the fans can be quite rough. Once Siva felt people grabbing his bum outside a radio station and other fans were taking pictures of the bum grabs. The photos ended up on Twitter for everyone to see!

The first time Nathan was asked to pose for a photo by a fan in the street was when he was visiting home. He was just walking along the high street and there were girls waiting outside shops for him. He was really surprised, as a few months previously he would have never imagined anything like that happening to him. All the boys don't see themselves as being super famous even though they are. They do realise that it is all down to the way they have treated their fans. Ever since they started out and performed for the first time the boys have taken time out to chat to fans and get to know them.

Max explained to the 3am girls, 'I think we've connected with people because we really make an effort with our fans. We meet them individually and give them a hug and a kiss. We're so grateful for their support.'

One of the biggest fan crowds in the early days was

when they did a signing for 'All Time Low' at London's Westfield shopping centre. Over 1,500 fans turned up and they queued for five hours to get the opportunity to meet the band. Nathan, Tom, Max, Siva and Jay were shocked to see so many fans turn up and were delighted to receive cards and gifts from some fans after they signed their CDs. They even got some knickers given to them.

Some fans can scare the band if they get too intense and won't let the band leave. Some girls chase the boys' van and won't stop screaming. They bang on the windows and try to get in. It's a good job that the boys travel around in a big van rather than a car, otherwise they could get flipped onto the side as fans pound the sides with their fists. They might get overexcited but who can blame them – Tom is often sat inside with his shirt off!

One fan took things a bit far as Max explained to the *Mirror*, 'We had one fan chasing after our car. She was clinging on to the door and licking the window. There were dead flies everywhere and the window was pretty clean by the time she was done.'

The weirdest request they have had from a fan so far has been when a Manchester fan asked them to sign her car door. The boys filled the whole door with a huge 'THE WANTED' and their signatures. They couldn't believe someone would want them to do that. In the

TOM POSES
FOR ANOTHER
PHOTOGRAPHER!

future that door would be worth a lot of money if the fan put it on eBay. The worst gift they've ever received was a used tampon which was thrown on stage whilst they were performing. The fan had written 'I love you' on it. That was an absolutely disgusting gift!

If you haven't been fortunate enough to meet The Wanted yet, have a read of Stacie Arme's story about the day she first met them. She is one of the band's biggest fans:

I first met The Wanted when they came to Trent Fm Radio Station in Nottingham on their radio tour. For some reason I was really nervous about meeting them. I got talking to some other fans whilst we were waiting for them to arrive and they were telling me that they are really nice and they just make general conversation with you. So that reassured me! When they finally arrived we saw them go into the lift to get interviewed and they were looking so good! We were waiting nearly two hours for them to come out but it was so worth it. Siva came up to me first and gave me a hug and then I got them all to sign a poster that my friend printed off for them to sign. I got a photo with Jay and I spent most of the time with him. He gave me a hug as well and his hugs are so good!! I said to him, 'Wow you smell nice!' and he said to me 'I was

Above: The Wanted: Jay, Nathan, Tom, Max and Siva. © *PA Photos*

Below: The boys out and about in Manchester. © *Wenn Images*

Cheeky Jay is probably
the most easy-going
member of The Wanted.

© *PA Photos*

Nathan is the youngest member of the band.

Tom once played Mark Owen in a Take That tribute band.   © *PA Photos*

Siva is the tallest
member of The
Wanted and has
a twin brother
named Kumar.

© PA Photos

Football mad Max is
from Manchester and
was formerly in a
band called Avenue.

© PA Photos

Above: The boys meet their adoring fans.

© *Wenn Images*

Below left and right: Max and Nathan during one of The Wanted's many live performances.

© *PA Photos*

Above: Tom and Jay have amazing stage presence.   © *PA Photos*

Below: Nathan and Siva sing harmonies during a live performance of 'All Time Low'.
© *Wenn Images*

actually just thinking the same about you!!' I was like oh! and my friend was just laughing with a shocked expression on her face. I didn't have a favourite member before that day but I left having a favourite member, and that's Jay. He was just so nice and friendly and he made me laugh and I made him laugh, and I loved that. I love people who can make me laugh and have a laugh with me as well.

Every time I meet them though I always seem to make a fool of myself in front of him! I met them on their 'All Time Low' CD signings as well. I went to the Nottingham signing and the Derby signing.

I've got to say the Derby signing was so much better than the Nottingham signing! I got a hug off Nathan and a hug off Jay. I made a complete fool of myself though because I cried in front of them! I still feel like a complete fool because I did that! Jay told me to hold his hand (so obviously I did) and he was saying that I am the sweetest girl ever! Now that's one thing that I can't get out of my head!

After the signing me and my friends Shanice and Nicole waited to see if we could meet the boys again and we were outside of the shopping centre and we were waiting for ages, and suddenly we heard screaming and we saw The Wanted's van coming down the road! So we pressed the button to cross the road and their van stopped at the traffic lights and we got to speak to them and they were throwing things out the van to us. I didn't get anything but Shanice got a water bottle, Tom's backstage pass to a concert they played at and Nathan's chocolate and Nicole got something from Max. It was such a good day! I really hope I get to meet them again some day. They are just five of the sweetest, funniest and most down-to-earth guys I have ever come across.

Fashion

The boys have a stylist who picks all their clothes for them and stops them making any fashion mistakes. In the past they have clocked up quite a few fashion mistakes as they explained to ASOS. Jay said, 'I only learnt not to do it this year but I used to straighten my hair. Looking back I look like a sissy girl. All I need is a bow to make it perfect.' Tom's biggest fashion mistake also relates to his hair. He told them, 'I had a shaved head, which made me look like a thug.'

Max's biggest fashion mistake is his snakeskin boots but this hasn't stopped him wearing them. People might point at them and laugh but he likes them. He says he's going to count how many people laugh next time he

CING T___ FRAGRANCE

wears them. Now he is a celebrity people will probably laugh less and might even think that he looks cool and buy a pair themselves.

The online clothing website also asked the boys what they like to see a woman wearing. They all replied 'Nothing' before Jay said the boho look, Max said jumpsuits, Tom said girly girls (which probably means skirts and dresses) and Siva said denim.

Max has the best clothes when he's not being styled. Tom has the second best, but that's because he steals Max's clothes. Jay has the worst sense of style but he doesn't need to worry about it now because their stylist always picks him out nice things to wear. Fans send the band nice things to wear too.

First Impressions

Everyone knows that it's important that when you meet someone for the first time that you give a good impression. When the band met each other for the first time it was a bit weird. Nathan, Tom and Jay had been picked first and then Jayne had picked Max and Siva to join them. Some of the band members had worked together during the audition stages but nothing prepared them for their first official meeting as the band.

Max wanted the other members to like him so he cracked lots of jokes to start with. He was trying really hard to be funny but in the end he just relaxed and let the real Max shine through. Jay felt intimidated by Siva's good looks at first but he doesn't now. Max likes to joke that Siva's identical brother Kumar is better looking than Siva.

For Siva it must have been exciting meeting the other band members but he might have been

MAX, THE JOKER
IN THE BAND!

SARAH OLIVER

wishing that Kumar was there with him. Kumar had
auditioned for the band too, along with another of
their brothers, but Jayne hadn't picked them. That
must have been hard for all three brothers – one got
to be in the band of his dreams and the other two had
to go home. Kumar and their other brother are still
supporting Siva and want him to do well. They would
have rather had one of them in the band than none of
them. Siva might have dropped out of the band if his
brothers hadn't been so supportive as he will always
have an unbreakable bond with his twin and the rest
of his siblings.

Aside from Siva, the other band members might
have also initially wished that some of the boys they
made friends with during the auditions had been
selected for the band, but they never talk about it in
interviews. Now, they realise that Jayne picked the best
five lads – and couldn't imagine anyone else being in
the band. They are all great friends and love working
and living together.

Food

They say that the way to a man's heart is through his
stomach and this is certainly true of the lads from The
Wanted. They love food.

Max loves pizza (Domino's especially) and The

79

Wanted's freezer always has some in so they can chuck a couple of pizzas in the oven if they get in late. He loves starting the day with a full English breakfast cooked by his Nan but now he's living in London he can't have it as often as he would like. If Max was going to a restaurant or a pub with the other lads he would probably go for a nice steak and chips, washed down with a pint.

Siva has a sweet tooth and he loves chocolate brownies. He likes home cooked Shepherd's pie and stew. Jay is like Max and loves a good pizza. He likes things that are easy to make like cheese toasties and chips. He can be a bit of a pig though and during the band's Habbo chat he ate 11 bags of Monster Munch. He just sat there munching his way through them as he answered questions.

Tom is the best cook in the house and he loves a good Chinese or Italian meal. He cooks for the rest of the band on a regular basis. He always does loads more than they need to, and there is always stuff leftover. He just chucks everything in a pan and creates really tasty meals that the others love.

Nathan describes himself as a horrendous cook and is by far the worst at cooking in The Wanted. When the boys had to do a *Come Dine With Me* style interview for the 519 show, Nathan was given the task of cooking the meal. It was a spoof of the cooking show so Nathan boiled chocolate bars and served them on a bed of spinach. It looked disgusting but the other lads stayed in character and pretended that they eat boiled chocolate bars all the time. It was very funny!

Nathan loves eating spaghetti bolognese and a good roast dinner but he can't have these very often as he hasn't got him mum to cook for him anymore. If he wants something he has to cook it himself or eat whatever the others have cooked. He says he can cook Pot Noodles but they hardly count because you just add hot water and stir. Since living with the rest of the band he has nearly blown up the kitchen by putting a tin of Heinz soup in the microwave. Oh dear!

When they are doing signings and performances they don't have time to eat proper meals. They end up eating lots of chocolate in their van and having cravings for weird food. Jay is partial to a scotch egg. Sometimes they throw chocolate out of their car's window for fans. Fans scream in excitement and keep the chocolate as if it's something worth a lot of money – they wouldn't dream of eating it!

Football

After singing, football is the band's passion. Max in particular is crazy about it. He is a huge Man City fan and if he could be any footballer for the day he would

Jay, during a performance of 'All Time Low'.

pick Carlos Tevez. Max told Popjustice, 'Yeah we're all into our football. Three of us especially but the other two are more into sort of music and stuff but I've twisted one of their arms into becoming a City fan.'

Max used to dream about being a footballer and would have loved to have played in Man City's first team. He's always been good at football and even played for England Schoolboys. His priorities changed when he was 16 and went on *The X Factor* with his boy band Avenue. Once they made the boot camp round Max realised that singing was what he really wanted to do.

Whenever he has a day off and Man City are playing he'll leave the rest of the boys in London and head up to Manchester. He loves going to derby games when Man City play Man United. They are the team he loves to hate. Whenever they play each other the house has to split in two because Nathan supports Man Utd. Nathan loves winding Max up when Man City lose in derby matches. When Paul Scholes managed to score the winning goal for Man U in the third minute of stoppage time during their 17 April 2010 match he was especially ecstatic because Max had gotten up at 6am so he could be there.

When The Wanted website went live someone made the mistake of putting on Max's profile that he supported Man Utd. He wasn't happy because they are the last team

THE BOYS LINE-UP FOR A PHOTO.

in the world that he would support – and it stayed on the website for a whole month before it was changed to Man City.

Max and Nathan love watching Match of the

Day on Saturday and Sunday nights. They can't get enough footy.

In May 2010 the boys took part in the Celebrity Soccer Six tournament at the Charlton Athletic FC football ground in South London. Lots of celebrities played in the tournament to try and raise as much money as possible for The Samaritans. McFly were there, Hollyoaks actresses, Big Brother contestants, Olly Murs and Stacey Solomon from *The X Factor* and loads more stars put on their football kits and boots. The boys played but things didn't go well – they were thrashed by a team from *The Sun* newspaper and their other games didn't go too great either. Back then our favourite team didn't have many supporters in the stands because 'All Time Low' hadn't been released so not many people knew who they were. Things will have changed by the 2011 Celebrity Soccer Six tournament because they will be one of the most popular teams on the pitch. TV presenter and former Arsenal and England star Ian Wright has already offered to play on The Wanted's team – Max is delighted. All the boys would love to play alongside such a legend, but it might be deemed a bit unfair on the other teams who won't have a former player on their side. We'll just have to wait and see what happens in May.

Jay is the complete opposite of Max and Nathan. He isn't into football at all, even though his whole family

MAX ON STAGE DURING A LIVE PERFORMANCE.

love the game. Jay's mum, sister and three brothers can't get enough football but all Jay wanted to do when he was younger and they all went to football practice was to stay at home and eat crisps. If he had to pick a team to support he would pick Celtic. Jay might have to have a few football practices before the next Soccer Six so he doesn't let the others down. Because there are only six players from each team on the pitch at once they can't afford to carry Jay. He needs to make sure his old childhood nickname 'banana kick' doesn't come back to haunt him. He might have never been able to kick in a straight line before but with a little bit of help from Max he should be okay.

Siva is the other member of The Wanted who isn't keen but Max has convinced him to support Man City. Tom, on the other hand, loves football and is a keen Bolton supporter.

Friends

Max has always loved going the pub with his mates and family for a pint (or three) on a Friday night. He can't do it as much now he lives in London but whenever he gets the chance he heads home to Manchester. His mates are so happy and proud of him that they don't mind that they hardly see him anymore. He can always stay in touch with them via text and emails though.

MAX GETS INTO A TAXI WITH A FRIEND AFTER A NIGHT OUT.

The two weeks around Christmas and New Year will always be a great time for Max, Tom, Jay, Siva and Nathan to catch up with the people who have been their mates for years. These are the people that the boys will be able to trust because they have known them for so long and before they were famous. Celebrities always have to be wary about who they let get close to them because some people will happily sell stories to newspapers – and paint the celebrity in a bad light.

As well as having their old friends the boys have made new celebrity friends since joining the band. They are very close to The Saturdays but can't see them as often as they would like because both bands are so busy all of the time. They get to meet up at concerts and award shows though.

Jay, Siva, Nathan, Max and Tom are all good friends but they do have the odd argument or two. This isn't surprising as they have very different personalities and they are with each other 24/7 as they spend all day in interviews or performing before heading back to their pad. They even go on holiday together!

G is for...

Geffen Records

The Wanted are on the record label Geffen Records. It is an American record label which is owned by Universal Music Group. Lots of very famous musicians and bands are or have been on the Geffen Records label. These include Aerosmith, Mary J. Blige, Guns 'N' Roses and The Saturdays.

Jay had been on the audition circuit for six months before he got in The Wanted so he must have been so thrilled when he realised that the label behind the band were so big. Geffen Records really believed in the boys right from the word go and they spent thousands and thousands of pounds in creating their sound and

TOM DURING A
PERFORMANCE OF
THE WANTED'S
NUMBER 1 SINGLE,
'ALL TIME LOW'.

producing their album. No expense was spared as they brought in the best songwriters to work with Nathan, Jay, Tom, Max and Siva. It was a bit risky to spend so much money but they had to if The Wanted were going to be a success.

Jay talked to Nokia Music about their record company shortly before 'All Time Low' came out. He said, 'When we first started, I genuinely didn't think about it (where the single would chart) at all. I just wanted to not embarrass myself and to contribute as much as I could. But the whole record company thing? They give you statistics of who's doing what in the same week as you, how many views you've had here, and just the expectations that they have puts you on edge. It goes straight to your head and you can't stop thinking about it. I really want a top 10, I have to say it. If we don't get it I will be gutted. But that's all part of it, though, isn't it? It's easy to be proud of people screaming at you or being in front of a crowd. But being able to tell your Dad, "I wrote that bit," that's dead good.'

All the boys felt under pressure before 'All Time Low' came out because they knew their whole futures depended on how well it did. Max knows only too well what it's like when a single flops and the record company calls the band in, only to tell them that it's over. He had to deal with the disappointment when that happened to

Avenue and so he was even more determined that it wouldn't happen with The Wanted. The boys put so much effort in to promote the single and will continue to do what they can to push all the other singles they ever do. They know they will never be able to put their feet up and become complacent because there are a dozen of other bands who want to be the Number One boy band in Britain.

Max revealed to Celebritain.com what being in the music industry is like: 'It's 100 miles an hour. It never stops and it never sleeps and it doesn't eat much either. We sleep in the car, we recline the seats and chill out and get an hour here and there. If we get four hours at home, that's a good night's sleep for us. We just run on adrenaline.'

Germany

In August 2010 the boys travelled to Germany for the first time. They didn't really know what to expect but were looking forward to promoting themselves and 'All Time Low' in a different country. They were all excited when they found out they'd be appearing on a huge German TV show whilst they were over there and introducing the singer Plan B. Taio Cruz was also going to be there so there was going to be a bit of a Brit theme to the show.

The night before they flew out they'd only managed to get two hours sleep because they'd been working on tracks for their album so they all tried to have a little nap on the plane. They knew they would have to be on top form because they'd be expected to speak a bit of German on every TV or radio show they appeared on. Once they arrived they tried to quiz their German driver and got him to translate things for them but they struggled to make what they were saying match what he was saying. Tom wanted to learn 'Where are all the girls' in German… but he didn't have time to try it out in real life. Max and Jay spent most of the flight and car ride doing impersonations of Siva which must have been really annoying. It's a good job that Siva is so easy going because their Irish accents would drive anyone up the wall.

The boys did a web chat for The Dome 55 but instead of German fans getting involved it ended up being mainly UK fans asking the questions. They did a performance of 'All Time Low' whilst they were there in the arena, on a huge stage in front of thousands of people. The boys usually get nervous before UK gigs but this was probably scarier because they didn't know how the German people would react to them. They needn't have worried because as soon as they came on stage everyone started screaming and hundreds of people tried to film them

NATHAN PLAYS TO THE CROWD DURING A PERFORMANCE.

on their mobiles. The stage was filled with smoke to start with and by the end they each had a flare and they were waving them around like they did in the video. It was an awesome night and one the boys will never forget!

Afterwards the German presenters tried to interview Max, Siva, Jay, Nathan and Tom but they couldn't because there was so much screaming going on. In the end the female presenter only got to ask one question and that was 'Have you seen anything of this beautiful city?' Max replied 'It's full of beautiful girls,' which made the audience scream even more.

Girls

The boys might seem confident on stage and in interviews but around girls that they fancy they can get a bit tongue-tied. Girls really confuse Nathan in particular and he doesn't understand why they love shopping so much. He would love to date a girl who likes having fun and is cute. He seems a lot less into picking girls with big boobs – unlike Tom and Max! The rest of the band think that Nathan is the band member most likely to date a fan in the future but that Tom probably would as well – he's girl crazy!

Nathan is the shyest member of the group when it comes to chatting up girls but he has quite a lot of female friends. His sixth form was in a girls' school so there were only about 15 boys and 120 girls. Max is probably the most confident and he has used chat up lines to get a girl's attention in the past but he doesn't need to now he's in the best boy band in the UK – gorgeous girls are coming up to him all the time and asking him out.

Because there is only Siva who has a girlfriend the others are available for dates but picking the right girl to ask out can be a problem. Jay confessed to the *News Of The World*, 'We do worry about what's going to happen with girls. You don't know their motives anymore. We've spoken to each other about that kind of thing. You feel stupid for thinking it but things have completely changed in the last few years. It used to be that you get caught from a dodgy photo but now people are publishing these texts – is nothing sacred anymore?!'

The boys can't afford for bad stories to come out about them. Even if an ex made up stories just to get a newspaper deal it could be damaging and lose them fans. They never want to do anything to upset their fans because their fans mean the world to them.

Another problem the boys face when they're chatting to girls is that they can never stay long in one place. They might see a nice girl that they fancy at a gig but after chatting for an hour they have to say goodbye and jump in their van. They can't go on proper dates because they are so busy right now.

The boys are always having weird conversations as they kill time between interviews and one day they decided to come up with the names they should have been called if they'd been girls. Jay thinks his name should have been Jane, Nathan opted for Natalie and Max went for Maxine. Tom wasn't sure but then picked Tamara and Siva thought that Sylvia would be a good girl's name for him. Since then they've played this game a few times and keep changing their girl names.

The boys don't mind that Siva has a girlfriend because they really like Nareesha. Plus it means that girls in clubs don't chase Siva because they know he's taken. Siva says he has met his perfect girl in Nareesha. They started dating before he got in the band and she's a shoe designer. Although they met in Belfast, she's originally from Nottingham. It must have been nice when Siva did a signing in the town because he was able to see where Nareesha and Jay grew up. They didn't get to see much of it though because it was the week 'All Time Low' came out so they had a full schedule. We'll have to wait and see if Siva and Nareesha manage to go the distance now the boys have hit the big time. It would be nice to see all of The Wanted at a wedding one day!

When Olly Meakings from *Teen Today* interviewed

NATHAN, TOM AND JAY SIGN AUTOGRAPHS FOR FANS.

the boys he asked them whether they would marry a fan. Jay said, 'In the future, I could marry someone who is or was ever a fan of The Wanted.' He told young fans (under 16) to not leave their personal details on forums and websites in the hope that a member of The Wanted would contact them because he knows it's not safe. If you are a fan and want to contact the band you can do it safely by writing to their fan mail address.

Siva also joked that he makes a note of all the phone numbers they are given and sticks them on his wall so that Tom can take his pick. This was just said in jest and he wasn't being serious.

Each member of the band is different so they each have different tastes in girls. Jay would like a girl who is fit, funny and friendly. He would like to date a girl who is good looking and has a great personality. If it was a girl whom he was hoping to have a long term relationship with it would be even more important that she had a great personality as 'looks fade'. If he just wanted a short fling looks would be more important.

Siva can describe his ideal woman (Nareesha) in three words: 'Mind-blowing, great cook.' Siva loves his food so he's so glad that she can cook him great meals. He's really good at baking chocolate brownies so he isn't afraid to make dessert. Tom and Max aren't that interested in girls that can cook; they like girls with big boobs and lovely legs. Max thinks tattoos are really sexy so he finds that girls with tattoos catch his eye. It depends on the tattoo though – a teddy bear one probably wouldn't be attractive to Max.

If you want to date the boys you might want to know what sort of date they would like to go on. Tom is a simple kind of chap and wouldn't want to go to a fancy restaurant for a meal – instead he'd like to go to McDonald's for a burger and some fries. Max's perfect date would be a Man City match but they'd have to win for it to be a good date. Afterwards he'd like a chippy tea – hardly romantic but at least you'd see what the real Max is like. Jay is really into his lizards so even if he didn't fancy a girl he'd still go on a date with her if she offered to take him to the reptile house at a zoo. Nathan and Siva would like a movie date. They like nothing better than chilling out with popcorn and a good movie.

Girls Can't Catch

Girls Can't Catch were a girl band that Siva, Nathan, Max, Tom and Jay were close to. The girl group was made up of Phoebe Brown, Jess Stickley and Daizy Agnew. Like the boys they were put together by a record company and Phoebe had appeared on *The X Factor* too (in the girl band Hope). Whilst The Wanted supported The Saturdays on tour, Girls Can't Catch supported Girls Aloud.

The five guys and three girls went to Loch Ness together and went exploring. They had great fun walking around, playing with a dog and seeing a mother duck with her ducklings. The boys must have been gutted for the girls when it was announced in July 2010 that they had been dropped by their record company and that Girls Can't Catch were no more. It must have hit them how easy it is for a record company to drop you if you don't make hit records. The girls only managed to reach number 26 in the charts with their first single 'Keep Your Head Up' and number 19 with their second (and last) single 'Echo'. The boys have already done much better than them in the charts but they will have to continue to make hit records to keep their record company happy.

Guy Chambers

Guy Chambers is a songwriting legend and most artists would give their right arm to get the chance to work with him. He is most famous for writing songs with Robbie Williams – they wrote the Robbie classics 'Angels', 'Millennium' and 'No Regrets' together. He has also penned songs for a whole host of other big

MUSICIAN GUY CHAMBERS.

names including Kylie, Beverley Knight, Mel C and Katie Melua.

When Jay, Nathan, Siva, Tom and Max heard that they would be working with Guy on their album they must have felt like pinching themselves. Guy doesn't normally work with boy bands, let alone new ones that haven't released anything yet. He only works with the best of the best so it was an amazing opportunity for the boys and one they will forever be grateful to their record company for arranging.

Guy was the first songwriter they worked with on the album so they didn't know what to expect. They were so happy that day but unbelievably nervous. It's a wonder any of them managed to sleep the night before. They soon relaxed once they met Guy and he got them to sing. It was a real privilege to get to sing for him and they soon realised that he's just a normal bloke. He isn't a diva, he enjoyed good banter with the boys and he invited them to his parties. Tom is a bit of a party animal so he knows the difference between a good party and a great party, and he thinks that Guy's parties are the best. They will all be hoping to work with Guy again on their second album because they loved working with him so much on the first album.

Siva decided to perform a song that he had written with his brother for Guy. He was so nervous but he managed to play his guitar and sing without fluffing up any of his lines. Guy listened and was more than impressed. He told Siva that they were going to record it!

Guy took Siva's song and made the harmonies so that the other boys could join in to. The song was still sung by Siva but Tom, Jay, Nathan and Max provided the 'oohs and aahs.' It was more than Siva had ever thought was possible.

H is for...

Heart Vacancy

'Heart Vacancy' was always going to be The Wanted's second single but they only got told it was definitely going to be released shortly before 'All Time Low' came out. They went all the way to Croatia to film the video and it took a few days to get it looking just how they wanted it to look. Siva liked 'Heart Vacancy' just as much as he liked 'All Time Low', even though it was a different type of track.

As soon as it was announced that 'All Time Low' was number one, Max, Siva, Jay, Nathan and Tom felt under immense pressure to get 'Heart Vacancy' to the top of the charts as well when it was released on 18 October.

They didn't want it to just make the Top 40, like they had wanted when 'All Time Low' came out – they wanted another number one!

In August 2010 two competitions were launched on the boys' official website relating to 'Heart Vacancy'. The first invited fans to pick a song for the boys to cover and the winning song would be dedicated to the person who suggested it and would be the B-side to 'Heart Vacancy'. The second competition was asking fans if they wanted to appear on the sleeve of 'Heart Vacancy'. One thousand lucky fans would be chosen and would see their names printed in the booklet that comes with every single. They were amazing competitions and many fans entered both within minutes of the message being posted.

Max told Celebrain before the official video came out: 'It's called 'Heart Vacancy' and it's slower, with a big beat… a ballad. It's one for the girls, but hopefully lads will like the beat in it.'

This track was written by Wayne Hector who co-wrote 'All Time Low'. It is an amazing ballad with really powerful, meaningful lyrics. It is definitely one of the best ballads of the last decade.

Holidays

The boys worked so hard promoting 'All Time Low' that they all decided that they needed a holiday

TOM SINGS HIS 'HEART' OUT DURING A LIVE PERFORMANCE.

together. They came up with the idea of going to Benidorm but had to keep it a secret from their management for as long as possible. They accidentally mentioned their plans during an interview with 95.8 Capital FM. The radio host didn't think they'd be allowed to go but Max told him 'We've booked it!' The boys did end up going but they were told to not get 'too brown in the face.' When they came back they had to go on GMTV so they were so tired. They had to be up at 4am. After their rehearsal Tom admitted that he's got the hots for Kate Garraway. They'll be going on more holidays together in the future but next time they'll be checking what they have to do the day after they get back. They won't be repeating the same mistake twice!

Hollyoaks

Being in the band has allowed the boys to do things they'd never thought possible. They were invited to perform on The *Hollyoaks* Music Show which was loads of fun. They sang outside Il Gnosh and there were loads of fans and stars there too. The actors who play Tom, Cheryl, Jem, Myra and Seth loved the boys and danced along to the music. Ellis Hollins, who plays Tom, even did some breakdancing whilst they were singing. The show aired for the first time on Saturday 12 June on T4 but it was repeated three more times. It was amazing for the boys to stand on the *Hollyoaks* set and meet the people they see on TV. They were all excited about meeting their favourite characters. Jay really likes Mercedes (played by Jennifer Metcalfe) and used to like Warren's little sister Katy (played by Hannah Tointon). Hannah's been in Doctors, New Tricks and a movie called The Children since leaving *Hollyoaks* – and she's in Cornetto and Clearasil adverts too.

The boys are big fans of the show and like to watch it when they can. It's trickier when they're on the road because they can't get home in time.

Home

Home is London for all five boys at the moment and it will remain this way for as long as they are in The Wanted. They have to live in London because that is where the recording studios and TV studios are and virtually everything they have to do apart from promoting their singles and album happens there.

Their first house was in the Wandsworth area of London and was a terraced property with five bedrooms so they could have one each. If it was for sale it would go for about £800,000 so the boys were lucky that their record company picked such a nice pad for them to live in. They could have been given a nasty

MAX AND A FRIEND SMILE FOR THE CAMERAS.

three-bedroom flat instead and have to share bedrooms. Their house had a lovely blue front door and it had a big living room and a big kitchen too.

The Wanted boys aren't the only famous people to have lived in Wandsworth. Former Prime Minister Tony Blair, tennis player Andy Murray and *Harry Potter* star Daniel Radcliffe have all considered Wandsworth home at some point in their lives. Take That's Mark Owen, former G4 member Jonathan Ansell and *This Morning* presenter Holly Willoughby are famous Wandsworth residents too.

Living together in Wandsworth was a big challenge at first for the boys as they didn't have their mums to look after them. They've slowly gotten better at cooking and cleaning up after themselves. Siva might be nicknamed Siva the Diva by the band's manager but he isn't really, none of the boys are. They have to do their own washing and dry their clothes on airers in their kitchen. Max and Tom are the messy ones and two cleaners have already quit on them. One cleaner was halfway through cleaning the house when she quit – and she hadn't even seen Tom's room which was right at the top. Nathan always has the tidiest room out of the five boys and will inspect his room before he goes to bed to see if anything needs tidying up – even if its two o'clock in the morning!

Because their first house was big they could each

have a double bed which was good because they could stretch out. It was especially handy when Max's dog came down from Manchester to stay for a bit. Elvis is a huge dog and his slobber can get everywhere. Dogue de Bordeaux dogs are really strong too so it's important they are trained from puppies to walk nicely on the lead otherwise they can pull you over. It must be so nice for Max when Elvis comes to stay but taking him for walks in the rain probably isn't fun. Max is really close to Elvis. It would be great if the boys could get their own permanent band dog but they are so busy it just wouldn't be practical. The only pet they could really have was a lizard so they got Neytiri who lived in a tank in Jay's room. Nathan told fans in a band newsletter, 'She has brought us several lasting memories, one of which was when she got onto the back of Siva's neck, he didn't like it and ran downstairs for us to get her off... Unfortunately, we didn't get there quick enough... Annnddddd she pooed all over him!!!! Gutted!!!'

Their house was in need of a feminine touch as the boys had loads of tough guy posters on the wall and there were no flowers or colourful cushions. Tom told The London Evening Standard during the promotional tour for 'All Time Low', 'We've got a dartboard on the door, fridge full of beer, freezer full of pizzas. What more do you need?'

If the boys had a night off and they didn't have to get up early the next day for something important Nathan would like nothing better than staying in, lying on his bed and watching a DVD or two. Tom and Max like to be out and about so would head for a club. They love having a drink and getting in really late. Nathan wasn't into that, partly because he is too young to go clubbing and, well, he likes to stay in!

Siva and Jay are stuck in the middle. Sometimes they like staying home with Nathan and watching a movie with him, other times they like going out with Tom and Max. It really depends on how they are feeling at the time.

Nathan does go clubbing when everyone else is going so he's not the odd one out. Bouncers let him in as long as he doesn't drink so he just has a J20 whilst the others have a beer. He must be excited about turning 18 in April 2011 because he'll be able to relax and have a drink if he wants without bouncers breathing down his neck.

Having to live together has allowed the boys to bond a lot more than they would have done if they had lived in different houses or hotel rooms. They get to see the best and the worst sides of each other. To prevent arguments they have their own set of mini house rules but Nathan and Tom can't help breaking them sometimes. They had to bring in rules so they could all get ready on time in the mornings. They have a '10 minutes only in the shower' rule but Nathan is forever breaking that one. The other four will be fully clothed waiting to get picked up and Nathan will still be running around in a towel trying to get ready because he's spent three hours in the bathroom. Tom's bad habit is getting milk out of the fridge and leaving it on the side – it really winds the other boys up. They always mention how annoying it is in interviews but Tom can't help it – it's something he's always done and his family back home have always had to put up with it.

Siva thinks that living in the house is just like being in college but instead of going to lessons they go and sing. They aren't having to live off a student's budget either, which is always good. It means they can order takeaway whenever they want without worrying about how they are going to pay for it. They are having the time of their lives. The boys always used to hang out in Max's bedroom in their first house because he had Sky and the others didn't.

The band had to leave their house in Wandworth on 14 August 2010 because their record company had found them an even better place to live. Normally bands get upgraded once a single takes off so it was a move that was expected by some fans of The Wanted. Movie actors experience the same kind of thing. When

Robert Pattinson started filming the *Twilight* movies he was in a hotel room with no windows and for the later movies he had his own suite of rooms. Who knows where The Wanted will be living in two years time after more hit singles, albums and tours?

Even though they were going to get a nicer place to stay Nathan was really sad. He tweeted: 'Loonngggg day people! Packed and moved out in a day! Dont move into the new place till September ... Soo ... I assume we're homeless now....!!'

Nathan had the most to do on that day because he didn't start packing until dinnertime and everyone had to be out by 5pm. He was supposed to pack up the bathroom whilst the others packed up the living room and kitchen but he left it until the last minute. Siva and Jay were the best at packing and made sure that all the photos and pictures they had received from fans were in a safe place so they could stick them on the walls of their new place. Tom was pretty lazy that day and tried to have one last lie in but he had to get up once people started banging things and moving the furniture.

In years to come the boys will probably return to the house, even if they have to stand on the street and just look at it from the outside because it is where The Wanted started out. It was in the house that they heard 'All Time Low' played on the radio for the first time and where they saw their first video on TV. They wrote some of their tracks for the first album there too. They had so many great times hanging out with fans outside and each other inside!

Nathan talked about his favourite memories of the band's time in the house during a newsletter he wrote to fans about the move. He said, 'We have also seen Jay locked in the basement, had estate agents peeking round our house to show people around while we were all sat watching TV in next to nothing. Had some hilarious and some quite awful practical jokes played on one another, for example Jay and Siva thought it would be a great idea to hide in my room while I was in bed for 10 minutes before they jumped out at me in the dark! Although I must admit it was all in revenge for me scaring them during a horror movie!'

He ended the newsletter by saying, 'So in many ways, moving house is the perfect way to end chapter one of The Wanted's life! We have had some amazing times and met loads of amazing people, including all of you who we have been lucky enough to meet!!!! Oh, and we also have got a NUMBER ONE!!!! So on to chapter two we go! On to a new house! New faces! The second single "Heart Vacancy", the album!!! But with chapter one complete, we would never be where we are now or be able to move on without all of you, the help we have had from the people we work with and the amazing support from all the fans! So I'm gonna leave this week's mailer as a massive THANK YOU to everyone who has been involved with chapter one!'

Seeing their belongings put in the back of a removal van was really tough and emotional for the boys as they were seeing their lives put into storage for a couple of weeks because they had to wait for a while until they could move into house number two.

I is for...

Inspiration

Everyone has people who inspire them and Siva, Nathan, Jay, Max and Tom are no different. They have been inspired by so many musicians and performers in the past and present. Because they have different musical influences this feeds into the songs they write and makes The Wanted's tracks so unique.

Tom would have never been in The Wanted if he hadn't picked up a guitar when he was 16. He'd never been interested in music before then, but once he started learning chords and playing songs he realised that making music was what he wanted to do. It was playing Oasis songs that inspired him to be in a band.

MAX LIGHTS UP THE STAGE DURING A LIVE PERFORMANCE.

Max isn't a typical Mancunian when it comes to his musical inspiration. He loves Queen and Elvis. Queen are a band that formed in 1971 and two of its members are still performing today. Their most famous band member Freddie Mercury died in 1991. Other artists and TV shows regularly cover Queen's songs, from *The Simpsons* to *Glee*. The band have had 18 number 1 albums, 18 number 1 singles and 10 number 1 DVDS. Max loves their songs so much.

Elvis is another strange choice considering that Max is only in his early twenties. He can't get enough of rock 'n' roll music and admits in interviews that he loves Elvis, and that it's a good job Elvis isn't still alive, otherwise people would think his Elvis obsession was even weirder than they do now. Max never says whether he likes 'Hound Dog', 'Suspicious Minds', 'Heartbreak Hotel' or one of Elvis's other tracks the most. It is estimated that Elvis recorded over 600 songs until his untimely death at the age of 42. That's a lot of music for Max and his other fans to enjoy.

Nathan's inspiration comes from listening to Boyz II Men tracks when he was growing up. Boyz II Men remain the best selling R&B group of all time and have won four Grammy Awards during their careers. They are an American group and first came out in the early nineties. They are still performing today. He likes the modern R&B music they produce, and he digs John Legend too. He thinks John Legend's 'Ordinary People' and Boyz II Men's a capella version of 'End of the Road' are great tracks and would encourage his fans to check them out.

Siva's biggest inspiration is the legend Michael Jackson but he also likes the American alternative rock band Switchfoot. Their biggest hits are 'Meant to Live' and 'Dare You to Move'. Their music was featured in the Mandy Moore movie *A Walk to Remember*. They are great guitar players and performers.

Jay has been influenced by so many people that he can't decide which have influenced him the most. He loves so many different types of music. He thinks Cat Stevens, Coldplay, Damien Rice, Newton Faulkner, Florence (from Florence And The Machine) and Jack Peñate are awesome singers and musicians.

Internet

Unlike some musicians whose fan base grows overnight (e.g. Susan Boyle and the *X Factor* stars), The Wanted have had to watch their fanbase grow at a much slower rate. They started having a few fans from their first school performance, and then they would do a big event and the next day get a few thousands more, then do a few school performances and get some more. Tom was shocked when they reached 10,000 fans on Facebook. He thought someone was having a laugh. The boys think that the hours they spend on Twitter and Facebook really help get people engaged with them. Jay thinks that their management would say that Tom is the best at tweeting because he's addicted to Twitter.

If they stopped tweeting the band would lose the connection they have with their fans. Because of this they would never stop – they enjoy the banter and getting feedback from fans. Some celebrities and musicians don't want to put the hours in on Twitter but for The Wanted this isn't an option – they love their fans so much and want to make them happy. When they are travelling it is so easy for them to send a few tweets as they can do it from their mobiles in a matter of seconds.

As well as normal fans on Twitter the boys have a few famous followers. *The X Factor* winner Joe McElderry, Chipmunk, The Saturdays and Tinie Tempah have been following the boys for months because they want to know what they are up to. In the next year many celebrities will start following Siva, Nathan, Max, Tom and Jay as they become personal friends of the band.

Rapper Tinie Tempah talked to MTV about how Twitter played a part in him getting to know the band and their music. He was also asked whether they could

rival JLS. He said, 'Yeah, every day on Twitter I would get loads of people asking me if I had heard about The Wanted and that I should check them out and we should do a track. I was thinking who are these guys and was like "not another boy band" but then I ended up tweeting "who are these guys The Wanted" and I'm quite honest on Twitter so if it looks like something is blowing up I will definitely touch on it and I got the opportunity to meet them at Summertime Ball at Wembley Stadium and they are the most down-to-earth guys, polite and respectful and they seem to have a huge following so why not and I wish them a whole load of success. As for JLS, I don't know why they can't both be around, their sounds are not the same and in the same way that you have Tinchy Stryder and Chipmunk I don't see why you can't have JLS and The Wanted. Let's celebrate and support it all, this is all British and we are at a point where we are dominating the charts and we are selling out shows. There is enough space for everyone.'

J is for...

Jay

Jay's full name is James McGuiness and he is 6'1" (the joint tallest in the band with Siva). His fans love his gorgeous curly hair, lovely blue eyes and amazing smile. He has a twin called Tom but they are not identical... they look pretty similar though. Tom has straight hair and is slightly smaller. They have a similar dress sense but have different interests. Tom likes football whereas Jay isn't interested in watching or playing soccer. They have two other brothers and a sister.

When *The Metro* asked Jay if he had ever had a psychic experience with his twin he replied, 'No. We were both sick on the bus at the same time on our first

day of school, though. We're not identical twins. That "psychic twin" stuff is just because you've had the same lives growing up. It's a load of rubbish.'

Jay spent his early years in the market town of Newark-on-Trent but then moved to a suburb of Nottingham called Carlton. He loved growing up in a city and it must have helped him deal with being in London once he got in the band.

Jay went to All Saints' Catholic School in Mansfield and enjoyed his time there but once he'd sat his GCSEs he decided that the time was right to move on. He didn't want to stay on and do A-Levels because he didn't want to go to university – he wanted to be a performer instead. He enrolled at MADD (Midlands Academy of Dance & Drama) which was in Carlton so he didn't have far to travel.

MADD was the best place for Jay as it was at the college that he developed his amazing singing, dancing and acting skills. The teachers at the college want every student to have a long and fruitful career in the theatre, TV or music. They couldn't be happier for Jay. Many former MADD students have gone on to appear as dancers for Girls Aloud, Take That, Westlife and Blue but Jay is the first to achieve a number one as a member of a boy band. It would be good if some of Jay's friends from MADD could be used as backing dancers when The Wanted tour.

Some people say that Jay is the Billy Elliot of The Wanted but he gets really embarrassed. He uses the excuse that he's the best because the others aren't very good at all but in all truthfulness Jay is an amazing dancer. Dancing has been his passion for a long time. Max might be passionate about footy but for Jay there is no contest.

Jay first started dancing when he was 13 which seems a strange age to start as most boys are starting to get into girls at that age and are very self-conscious – they don't want to seem uncool. It's not known if Jay kept the fact that he went to dancing classes with his mum a secret – but he soon became obsessed with dancing.

Jay told the *Metro*, 'My whole family are football nutters – I wasn't at all. I was a little fat kid who watched television. My mum was injured playing football and went to a tap-dancing class to stay fit. I went along with her, started dancing, enjoyed it and wanted to try to do it as a job when I'd finished my GCSEs.'

After graduating from MADD, Jay was even more eager to make it and so started auditioning for as much as he could. It must have been horrible going for auditions and being told he wasn't what they were looking for. He wouldn't give up though and kept going to audition after audition for six whole months before his first audition for The Wanted. Looking back now he will be so glad that he kept getting told no but at the time it must have knocked his confidence. It's hard to picture the band without Jay in the line-up, he makes a big impact in interviews and during performances. He is the cheeky chappy from Nottingham whom we love.

At first Jay thought he wanted to be a dancer so he mainly auditioned for dancing jobs. He had the moves people wanted but they didn't think he looked right. They wanted dancers who were bigger built and looked tough rather than like the guy next door. Jay realised this and so tried to think of other things he would like to do. He did a circus audition (but didn't get the job) and then tried out for a new boy band (The Wanted).

He talked to Industry Music about how he isn't your average dancer: 'Thing is I'm not like the other dancers – they were all into R&B and I'm into indie and Jack Peñate, Cat Stevens, stuff like that. That's why I'm glad I found the other lads. It's like I finally make sense now.'

Jay has got four pet lizards and can play the piano a bit but he's nowhere near as good as Nathan.

All The Wanted boys are quite mischievous but because they work so much they don't always have time to put their prank ideas into action. Tom revealed on a Wanted Wednesday video that he and Jay had been planning on putting some bacon into Siva's shoe and leaving it for a few months until it smelled really bad but that they hadn't got around to it. Tom has a fear of fish that he doesn't like talking about so Max liked the idea of putting a kipper under his bed but again he hasn't done it yet.

The other band members think that Jay is the most easygoing person in the world. He never stresses and just takes things in his stride. When they have meetings with their stylists he doesn't feel the need to kick up a fuss if they've picked out something he doesn't want to wear. If they didn't have a stylist Jay would have the worst clothes out of the band – but he'll happily put his hands up to not having much fashion sense. Max went as far as to say during one Wanted Wednesday video, 'You could be doing the marathon naked, running on broken glass but if you said "Jay, I really want you to do it with me" he'd be like "Alright then."'

Being in the band is a dream come true for Jay and he still can't believe famous people and musicians rate their music. One day he tweeted: 'Craig david went past our dressin room and said well done! Get in!!!'

He loves being able to spoil his mum Maureen and the rest of his family but he is making sure that he doesn't spend every penny he earns. On 7 August he tweeted '@Carly_Lew have a wicked birthday! it's my little bro's birthday today as well! his birthday present is sliiightly better than last years ;)'

It's important that all the boys learn how to save so that they will be able to buy their own houses or apartments one day. They don't want to waste it all and have nothing left to show for it.

THREE FASCINATING FACTS ABOUT JAY

- He took on the challenge of Bop It during one interview and managed to complete it in 3 minutes 18 seconds. No one expected him to be able to go for that long, Max even put his head on the desk and rested his eyes. Jay was still going when it said 'High Score 250'. That was the first time that anyone in the room had ever seen the game completed.

- He has a phobia of polystyrene and one night Siva thought it would be funny if he put some under Jay's pillow. Jay woke up and was shocked to find Siva's surprise. Jay has said in the past, 'The act of pulling polystyrene out of a box is totally repulsive. It just makes me shudder.'

- He loves eating crisps, but once he opens a bag he can't stop. He gets fed up with the junk food they have to eat when they're travelling in their van but he can't do anything about it.

Jayne Collins

Jayne is the manager of The Wanted and she is the woman who acts like a surrogate mum to Siva, Nathan, Max, Tom and Jay. She is the one the boys turn to for advice and she makes sure they always get to where they need to be at the right time. Without Jayne the band would have never been put together as she selected each member. She is helped by Lori and Dan.

Jayne might have worked with a lot of famous bands and recording artists over the years but she thinks The Wanted work harder than anyone else. She is so impressed by their attitudes and the way they always put 110% into everything they do. Quite often her two young children will accompany Jayne when she's helping the band move house or when they're going to a special event. She is a fantastic manager and a fantastic mum at the same time. The boys must enjoy joking around with Jayne's kids and making them laugh.

Jayne is a casting director and she's always looking for new talent. If you want to be a singer, actress or actor you should search for 'Jayne Collins Casting' on Facebook and join the group that Jayne has set up. It lets you know when she's looking for people for bands or for other projects.

Jayne has advice for young people wanting to make it in the music or TV world. She told 1click2fame.com, 'Presenting yourself is hugely important. Being on time, knowing the script or the dance you are to perform. Having a CV with your photograph with your name written on the back of the photograph. These all sound like little things, but they are hugely important.

'If you want to be the best, you want to be the most successful and that means hard work. Putting in the work before you become famous is probably the best advice.'

Jayne knows what she is talking about as she was a singer and actress herself. She appeared on the hundredth Baywatch episode as an aspiring pop singer alongside Richard Branson. In the episode she saved his life as he tried to break a world record so he let her record her own track 'No Turning Back'. The song was great and Jayne sounds a bit like Kylie on the track, but it only managed to get to number 102 in the UK. She released other songs and had quite a few fans, but not as many as The Wanted have. Now she is happy just being a manager and a casting director. She gets a bit embarrassed when Jay or Tom mention her Baywatch past. They love telling their fans to check out her videos on YouTube, and many do and leave nice messages for Jayne underneath.

Jayne loves hanging out with The Wanted and always makes sure that she films them behind the scenes so fans don't miss out on anything. The videos are used to make Wanted Wednesday videos and she posts them on The

Wanted's YouTube channel. Jayne doesn't put every video up (just the highlights) but it would be nice if one day all her recordings could become an official *The Wanted Behind The Scenes* DVD movie. She captures everything they do – Jay even jokes she's filmed him going the toilet a few times... she hasn't really though. If you want to follow Jayne on Twitter you can; here is the address you need: http://Twitter.com/jaynecollinsmac. She is forever sending the boys messages and they always send lovely ones back to her telling her they are looking forward to seeing her when they wake up.

Jayne tried to film behind the scenes when the video for 'All Time Low' was being made but when she let Jay have a look he accidentally deleted what she had taken. She had to start again so she wasn't pleased. Another time Jay's lizard ran over the flip phone when he was exercising it and the lizard's feet managed to wipe all the videos. It's a good job Jayne's a patient woman!

JLS

The media might see JLS as the boys' biggest rivals but the two bands don't have a problem with each other. They actually rate each others music very highly. Max, Siva, Tom, Jay and Nathan think that JLS are great guys and love being compared to them. The Wanted and

JLS really need to stick together to take on the girl bands who have dominated the charts for the last few years. It's time for boy bands to show how talented they are!

THE WANTED HAVE A LOT OF RESPECT FOR JLS AND LOVE BEING COMPARED TO THEM.

Max explained how the band feels to Popjustice: 'I don't see ourselves as rivalling JLS, I mean JLS have absolutely smashed it. So fair play to them, like. We just wanna do what we do. We just want to be ourselves, know what I mean? We just want to get on with it and see how we get on.'

Jay thinks comparing The Wanted with JLS is 'Like comparing *Avatar* to *Lord of the Rings* – just don't do it,' he told *Teen Today*. 'They're good in their own right but they're in different genres, they might be similar i.e. fantasy/boy bands but I think they're very different and complement each other. I'm a die hard fan of both!' Everyone knows that Jay is a huge *Avatar* fan so can understand why he got all passionate when he was explaining the bands' situations using his favourite movies as an example. Everyone else seemed to be very confused in that interview.

People might think JLS wouldn't like a new boy band on the scene, let alone one getting a number one debut single but this couldn't be further from the truth. Aston, Marvin, JB and Oritsé have been offering the lads some advice and don't have a problem with them at all. The Wanted think JLS are great and admire their dancing skills. Max and Tom think they might need to try and have some dancing lessons – Max even tried to do a flip like the JLS boys do but he couldn't pull it off. Thankfully he was on his own at the time!

Lots of The Wanted's fans love both bands equally so it would be nice if they could do a tour together one day. They could even release a song together for charity like Girls Aloud did with the Sugababes. Thousands of fans would rush out and buy the track and they could raise thousands of pounds for a worthy cause.

Jobs

The boys have the best jobs in the world right now but their lives could have been so different if they hadn't decided to audition for Jayne Collins. They all turned up and impressed from the outset so Jayne had to invite them back. She knew all five of them were very special from the very beginning.

Before auditioning for the band, four out of the five boys were going nowhere fast. Jay was going to dance auditions and not getting any jobs so he had to work as a waiter and a key ring seller in nightclubs just to get by. The girls he served in the clubs must be kicking themselves now if they recognise him on TV, they'll be thinking, 'Why didn't I get his number?' They could be dating a superstar if they had!

Max had in some ways given up his pop dreams and was playing football and signing on the dole. Nathan was still in school so he was busy with homework and exams. He probably thought it would be years before he got his first proper full-time job. Poor Tom was stuck working in McDonald's.

Only Siva was going places as he was modelling for Storm Model Management with his twin Kumar. In March 2009 they featured on The Ones2Watch website because people in the modelling industry thought that they were the next big thing. That said, Siva was still working in a museum between modelling jobs.

If the band ever split up Siva, Tom, Max, Jay and Nathan would quite like to be managers and casting agents like Jayne Collins. They think she has a great job and they'd like to help put bands together. They would make great mentors to a new band because they have been there themselves. They know what it's like when you first start out and you are waiting to see how your first single charts.

Tom has different job ideas to the others. He admitted in a Wanted Wednesday video that he would have liked to have been a footballer if he wasn't a singer but that it would have never had happened because he wasn't good enough to be a professional player. He thinks being a bin man would be fun or taking photos for *Nuts* magazine or *The Sun*. He loves girls so much!

K is for...

Kisses

Some members of The Wanted might dream of kissing a celebrity but Nathan has already done it. He was kissed by one of the most famous women on the planet when he was still in primary school. Nathan told Bliss magazine, 'I kissed Britney Spears when I was 10 and performing on Saturday morning TV. All my friends at school were so jealous!' The kiss made Nathan a legend in his school and everyone wanted to be friends with the lad who kissed Britney.

Jay kissed one fan on the lips for ages because it said on the back of her drawing that she wanted a snog. It was filmed so if you want to check it out, head over to

NATHAN KISSED
BRITNEY WHEN HE
WAS 10 YEARS OLD!

The Wanted's YouTube channel. Once this happened lots of fans must have tried writing similar messages on their drawings in case Jay decided to carry on fulfilling his fans' wishes.

Some fans don't just want to kiss the boys, they want to marry them. On the day they were leaving their first house Jay opened some fan mail from a very, very young girl. She had written about how they were going to fall in love and what their wedding would be like. Jayne was filming Jay at the time but instead of saying it was silly or laughing he just smiled and said it could happen, you never know. This shows how lovely and kind Jay is. He's one in a million!

L is for...

Lady Gaga

Out of all of the artists that are big at the moment it is Lady Gaga that the boys admire the most. This seems like an unusual choice as the majority of Lady Gaga's fans are girls. Max doesn't just like her music, he finds her really attractive too. The boys have never met Lady Gaga in the flesh but they will get to one day as they are bound to bump into each other at Awards shows. Maybe Max will understand what it's like for his fans when they meet him, because he'll have to be brave and go up to Lady Gaga if he wants her autograph or a photo.

Tom admires Lady Gaga for her songwriting abilities because she doesn't just sing songs other people have

written for her. She actually wrote songs for other artists before she landed her record deal.

Jay shares Max and Tom's admiration for Lady Gaga and told 4Music, 'She's got everything: she writes it all, she's an amazing singer and performer, and she's got the cash to make amazing videos and amazing shows.'

The boys might like her videos but they must be glad that their stylist never makes them wear crazy outfits like Lady Gaga wears. They just get to wear normal clothes that don't make them stand out too much.

Loose Women

Being in the band has allowed the boys to visit virtually every radio station and TV station in the land. They have been on young, hip TV shows and ones for the more mature woman. They loved being interviewed and performing on *This Morning* and *Loose Women* because they knew how much their mums and nans like the shows. Siva in particular liked doing *This Morning* because he got to talk about Ireland with presenter Eamon Holmes.

Max talked about their first visit to the *Loose Women* set to Celebritain.com: 'Nathan sort of tapped Kate (Thornton) on the shoulder to give her a kiss but as he did that, she turned round with her mouth gaping and almost swallowed Nathan's head.'

The boys did really well during their interview and answered all the questions Kate, Denise Welch, Sherrie Hewson and Jane McDonald asked them. Max thought they all looked hot in an older woman type way.

When he was asked by the Celebritain.com journalist whether any of the women were giving him the eye he replied, 'Oh yeah, Jane McDonald was giving me the eye. They were all at it. Good job Carol wasn't there!'

Kate, Denise, Sherrie and Jane must have loved having five gorgeous lads to interview for a change. They will no doubt be seeing the boys every time they release a new single. Everyone wants them to appear on their show, so soon there won't be a presenter in the UK that they haven't met.

M is for...

Max

Max was born in Manchester on 6 September 1988 in Hope Hospital, Salford. He was given the name Maximillian Alberto George by his parents. It was too long-winded so he soon became simply Max. He is the second oldest member of The Wanted (after Tom) but is the smallest as he's only 5'8".

Max went to Broad Oak Primary School in the East Didsbury part of Manchester. The teachers were really strict at playtimes and the school had a 'no ball' rule. Footy mad Max had to make do with stones for footballs and him and his mates would kick them around instead. The stones left horrible bruises on Max's legs where they

hit him – his mum wasn't pleased but he couldn't help it. He needed to play football, he couldn't be one of those kids who just spent breaks walking around the playground chatting.

Max wanted to be a professional footballer even then but had to give up on his dream a few years later when he got a serious injury. He told Industry Music, 'I snapped my hip flexor – the muscle that joins your groin to your hip. That pretty much ended my football career.'

This broke Max's heart as he was such a talented player and he could have gone all the way. He even played for Manchester City, Bolton and England Schoolboys. Some of his former team mates are playing for some of the biggest clubs in the Premier League and earning megabucks.

Rather than sit around moping, Max decided to try something new and found out that he really enjoyed singing and performing. He joined the boy band Avenue and for a while he thought he had found his place in life. They auditioned for *The X Factor* and got through to the final 12 before they were disqualified because they had broken the rules. It was during a meeting with Louis Walsh when they had to sign a management contract that the band had to admit that they already had a management contract with someone else. Max and his bandmates hadn't realised that having a management deal in place broke the rules and were left feeling shell-shocked when they were told they had to leave the show and wouldn't be doing the live shows.

This was another big blow to Max but rather than giving up on being in the music industry the band decided to keep going, and after replacing one member, got the record deal that they had been yearning for. They released a single called 'Last Goodbye' in September 2008 but it only reached number 50 and they didn't get to release another one and their tour was cancelled.

Max took some time out when they split in April 2009 but it wasn't long before he was auditioning for bands again and he decided to try out for the new band Jayne Collins was putting together. Max must hate it when the media try to say that The Wanted are the same as Avenue because they are completely different. He feels so much closer to Tom, Jay, Siva and Nathan than he ever did to Johnny, Jamie, Scott and Ross even though he was in Avenue for three and a half years. If he could turn back the clock he would still have joined Avenue because he learnt so much from being in a band and it has helped him deal with things better now he is in The Wanted. He talked to Popjustice about how things have changed for him: 'I think this time I've learned to put more in myself rather than being told what to do by people. It's good to have your own involvement, get your views across and your opinions, because at least if you can say your opinions, they don't have to listen but at least you've put it forward. Even when we didn't want something (in Avenue) we didn't speak up. With this one we write our own songs in this group and we didn't do that before.'

Having a second chance to be a pop star has made Max so happy and he isn't going to let anything ruin things for The Wanted. He wants them to be around for years and years. He confided to the *Manchester Evening News*: 'I just feel really lucky to be honest, because I know a lot of people try really hard and it doesn't always happen for them in this business. I never wanted to give up on my dream, but I pretty much said this would be my last chance with a boy band, and it looks like it's paid off.'

His family are so happy that things are going right for Max and they think the other boys are great. It would be awful for any of the boys if their parents didn't like the other members, but they have all been adopted into the George, Sykes, McGuiness, Parker and Kaneswaran families.

When Max took Jay to meet his family, his Nan decided to do them a fry up. Max had to explain to his nan that Jay is a vegetarian. She said to Jay, 'Never mind, dear.' This cracked the boys up and Jay told their manager Jayne that she said it 'like it was a terminal illness.' Jay didn't go hungry though, Max's nan did him a plate of eggs instead.

Sometimes Max's dad drives the band around Manchester when they are in the city but he doesn't seem to mind. It must be nice for him to have Max home.

THREE FASCINATING FACTS ABOUT MAX

- Max met Michael Jackson! Jay wishes he had – and says that when Max talks about it, he gets goose pimples!

- He loves playing with people's ears and making them sing. He puts on a CD and then makes a lips shape with someone's ear and moves it so it looks like the ear is singing. Weird but true!

- He loves lizards, just like Jay. When he was in Avenue he had six lizards but now he shares a house with The Wanted lads they have one lizard between them.

Media training

Record companies always insist that their artists have some form of media training before they can do any interviews. They need to be confident that the artist can give the correct answers without having to think long and hard before answering. Sometimes interviews are only a couple of minutes long so there isn't any time for hesitation.

The Wanted went along to media training and found it really useful. Their trainer got them to pretend that they were having a radio interview and fired questions at them. He started off giving them easy questions so they could get the hang of replying super fast but then tried trickier ones.

If you watch video interviews of the band promoting 'All Time Low' you can see that Jay is normally the one who answers questions about what the song is about and that Nathan answers the questions about why they are called The Wanted. They seem to have sorted out who is going to answer what beforehand as it's very rare for the band to speak over one another. Their media trainer helped them so much that they are always so relaxed in interviews and don't stress about what to say. Obviously they don't have a script but they always have some idea of what is going to be asked.

The best interviews are the ones when the interviewer asks a wacky question that no one has ever asked the band before. They have to think on their feet and answer quickly so sometimes the answers they give are really funny.

Mobiles

Being a celebrity and keeping your private life private can be a challenge. Stars don't want their mobile numbers being passed around so that anyone can ring them at any time of the day or night. They only want their close friends and family to be able to contact them 24/7.

The Wanted are no different. Each member of the band has a normal phone and at least one dummy phone so they can give that number out to people they have just met or girls they fancy. That way they can keep their normal phone's number private and stop it getting into the wrong hands.

Modelling

Back in June 2010 Siva, Max, Tom, Nathan and Jay performed at The Clothes Show London but they had to share a changing room with the models. This was quite tricky because the models only had a few seconds to get into their next outfit so they just ran in and stripped off before running out again. The boys had to try and avert their eyes as these naked girls ran past. Siva was used to it because he's been a model so knows what it's like. It was probably hardest for Tom not to look because he loves girls so much!

Everyone thinks that being a model is an easy job but

NATHAN STRIKES A
POSE DURING A LIVE
PERFORMANCE.

it isn't. You are used like a canvas and the designer will change your appearance just to make you look the way they want you to look. They can dress you in silly outfits but you can't complain. During one modelling shoot Siva had to wear some glittery pants, no top and sandals… and he had a weird ball structure over his head too. It was supposed to look cool but it was very odd. He's so glad he does music instead of modelling now.

In August 2010 all the boys got to be models for a day because they were shooting their first ever calendar. They probably hadn't thought about the possibility of doing calendars when they first started out, but their management and record company realised that thousands of girls would love to start every month of 2011 with a new picture of the band on their wall. Jay got to pose in a Mini Cooper during the shoot and would have loved to have been allowed to keep it. Fans wanted the band to show off their muscles in some pictures and to do some photos of them looking all cute and kissable.

Muscle

As the boys have become more and more famous they have had to get more and more paid muscle to protect them. They need their own security people to help them travel from their car to a venue as crowds will often try to push their way to the boys. This might seem harmless to some people but it can be dangerous. The boys could get crushed or if a fan fell on the ground they could get trodden on and hurt. The Wanted don't want this to happen so they have their own security people to hold back the crowd and make a safe passage for them.

Having to walk around with security men is something that the boys are going to have to get used to because the more famous they get the more security men they will need. The security men also help keep the paparazzi at bay.

The Wanted always want to sign autographs for their fans and at one performance at the Westfield Shopping Centre they stayed for five hours to sign autographs. Fans were handed different coloured wristbands and asked to leave in groups to prevent a scrum. The security men are very experienced and can deal with any situation as they are former SAS soldiers.

TOM SHOWS OFF HIS MUSCLEY ARMS OUTSIDE A PARTY.

N is for...

Naked

Max has posed naked for a magazine in the past. It was to raise awareness for Cancer Research and to try and encourage men to check themselves for lumps. Max was completely naked apart from an Avenue road sign. He didn't seem to mind because it was for such a good cause. Maybe in the future Siva, Nathan, Tom and Jay might be willing to do the same kind of thing. The Wanted fanbase would be over the moon if they did!

Max and Jay say that Tom always strips off in the car and sits there naked. Nathan is usually the one behind the camera when videos of the boys running around half naked are made. The rest of them come out of their rooms and don't expect to see Nathan stood filming them. Other times he sneaks into their rooms when they are asleep and films them so fans can see what they are like when they're sleeping.

When the band decided to take some photos in a photo booth at a railway station they caused a stir because Max and Tom stripped off and lots of people were waiting outside for their turn. When they'd finished a man went in and drew the curtain – and the boys couldn't stop laughing because a picture of them naked was on the screen. The man inside the booth must have been so confused. If you want to see the photos of the boys head over to their official website www.thewantedmusic.com as the background is made up of their photo booth shots.

Nathan

Nathan James Sykes (or Nate as his mates like to call him) was born on 18 April 1993. He grew up in the Abbeydale suburb of Gloucester and is the youngest member of The Wanted. He says he is 5'9" but the boys' manager Jayne thinks he's smaller than that. Because he's not very tall he wouldn't want to date someone who was taller than him because it would make him feel even smaller than he is.

He has one younger sister and lived with his mum

before moving down to London to live with the boys. His dad doesn't live too far away and is so proud of Nathan. Nathan told his local newspaper what happened when he told his sister he was in the band: 'When I first went home and told Jess I was in a boy band she thought it was quite funny, she said I had no street cred because I was in a "boy band" but I think she has been convinced now. She is really happy for me and I am hoping I have a bit of street cred back now.'

Unlike Tom, who only got into music when he was 16, Nathan has been musical since primary school. He first sang on stage when he was six and loved every minute. He was born to perform. He first started playing the piano when he was seven and is a really good pianist now, even though he says his little sister is better. In 2002 he appeared on the Britney Spears *Karaoke Kriminals* TV show and came in first place. He won a signed photo of Britney, a trophy and a skirt she wore in the movie *Crossroads*. It was an amazing achievement because so many children applied to be on the show. Two years later Nathan decided to go on ITV's *Ministry of Mayhem* when they did an *X Factor* style competition. In 2007 he won The Door's Undiscovered Youth Talent Competition in Stroud with a spine tingling performance of 'Mack the Knife' from *The Threepenny Opera*. Nathan continued to sing and perform and the following year at the age of 14 he made it to the regional rounds of Live and Unsigned. He might not have made it any further but he still did well to get to the stage he did. He also won The Cheltenham Competitive Festival of Dramatic Art twice, in 2003 and in 2008.

Despite having a passion for singing and appearing in so many different talent shows, Nathan has never let it affect his school work. He went to Longlevens Junior School which wasn't far from his home. It was a big primary school with over 400 students. He was going to go to The Crypt which is a selective boys grammar school next but when he was offered a scholarship at Sylvia Young Theatre School in London he couldn't say no. The school is a specialist performing arts school and so many famous people have been students there. Billie Piper, Emma Bunton, Amy Winehouse and Vanessa White are just four of over fifty big stars who learnt their craft at Sylvia Young Theatre School. Going to the school was a challenge for Nathan because his family didn't live in London. He had to travel for three hours every day just to get there, and then it would take him another three hours to get back. Getting up at 5am every day must have been so tiring for Nathan but he was willing to do it to get the opportunity of a lifetime.

After attending Sylvia Young Theatre School Nathan decided that he wanted to do A-Levels so he would have something to fall back on, so he went to Ribston

Hall High School in Gloucester for the sixth form. His new classmates had no idea that he was a talented singer because Nathan didn't tell them. He had been going to auditions to get in the band but couldn't tell anyone when he was actually told by Jayne that he was in the final line-up because it had to be a big secret. He revealed to his local paper that he finally came clean at a talent contest: 'I thought it was for charity, so I said I'd do it. I was saying for weeks that I was going to do it, but they thought I was joking. Then I got up on stage and they were all shocked that I could sing.' Nathan managed to do his exams shortly before 'All Time Low' came out but he won't be able to do his final year at Ribston because he will be too busy touring and releasing more singles. The school have said that he can return whenever he wants. He probably won't need to now he's a megastar.

Nathan might be the youngest but he acts like an old man sometimes and can be the most sensible in certain situations. Before doing anything he likes to sit down and have a cup of tea. Whenever one of the other members of The Wanted is making themselves a cup of tea he always asks if they'll make him one too – he loves tea! It doesn't matter if he's running late, he's always got time for a cuppa.

Nathan's dad Harry spoke to the *Citizen Reporter* shortly after 'All Time Low' became number one. He said, 'I'm extremely proud of him. From my point of view, Nathan has worked tirelessly to achieve this goal ever since the age of six. He has been wowing crowds for years, and now he's performing to hundreds of thousands of people.

'The joy running through the family here and up in Grimsby where my side of the family is from was amazing. Everybody's proud of him. We've been supporting him and going to see some of his concerts.'

Nathan must have been gutted that he couldn't celebrate with his family the night Radio 1 announced that 'All Time Low' was number one in the charts. The next day he decided to nip home to see his mum and sister, and they had a small family party. He is super close to his mum and sister and rings them every day to let them know what he's been up to. Whenever things get too much he knows that he can call his mum up and she can give him advice. He thinks he wouldn't be in the band if it wasn't for his mum because he thinks that the fact that she is a music teacher made him want to do music. Nathan's trip home only lasted a day but he was so glad he went.

He told the *Citizen Reporter*, 'I always wanted to do singing as a career even though people would tell me it was really difficult to get into, and I was prepared to put in a lot of hard work to do what I wanted. I hoped I would be number one when I was younger but I never thought it would actually happen, when I was younger I was quite quiet and shy but on stage I am completely different.'

THREE FASCINATING FACTS ABOUT NATHAN

- If the band split up they all think that Nathan will be the one who goes solo because he's so talented.

- In 2004 Nathan was in a competition on TV to find the act to represent the UK in the Junior Eurovision Song Contest. He came third with the song 'Born to Dance'.

- If he was getting married and he had to pick one member of The Wanted to be his best man he would pick Max because he would give a good speech.

Above: The Wanted line up for a photo.   © *Wenn Images*

Below: Jay meets fans during a live performance in London.   © *Wenn Images*

Jay and Siva play to the crowd.

Nathan (above) and
Max (right) have
always loved to sing
and make music.

© PA Photos and
© Wenn Images

Tom smiles at fans during a performance at Westfield Shopping Centre in London.

Max enjoys himself whilst performing live.

Above: Siva performs in Blackpool.

© *Wenn Images*

Below: The boys begin another song during a gig in Westfield Shopping Centre in London.

© *Wenn Images*

O

is for...

Originality

Every band wants to be original with their music and their name. They don't want to copy other bands; they want to be trendsetters.

Writing and singing original songs was very important to Siva, Nathan, Max, Jay and Tom and they are so glad that their record label didn't make them release a cover for their first single. They would have hated to be like the *X Factor* winners who have to release a cover, and people always compare their version to the original. With 'All Time Low' this didn't happen because The Wanted were the first people to sing it.

Picking a great sounding original name was very

important too. If they had picked a rubbish name then people might not have taken them seriously. Nathan was the one who came up with the name The Wanted and the others all agreed that it was a cool name. Some people have said that they should have called themselves Wanted rather than The Wanted but this wasn't an option. There was already a New Jersey country, rock and blues band called Wanted who have been performing together for the last twenty years. Bands can't use a name if another established band is already using the name. In 2002 the band Liberty had to change their name to Liberty X after a complaint was made by a band called Liberty and they lost a court case.

Nathan told the *Daily Star* how he came up with the name: 'We've got a song called 'Let's Get Ugly' and it samples a tune from *The Good, The Bad And The Ugly*. I had this vision of us all on one of those wanted posters and because the lads couldn't come up with anything better, it stuck.'

P is for...

Performing

All the boys love the opportunity to perform to any size of crowd. They all have particular towns and cities that they enjoy performing in the most. Jay loved performing in Nottingham because his friends and family came to watch. It made it extra special to see them in the crowd wearing Jay t-shirts and holding banners. It probably made him more nervous at first but once he started to sing he would have forgotten anyway and just concentrated on singing 'All Time Low' the best he could.

Max agreed with Jay and thought their performance at Nottingham's Royal Concert Hall was the best gig they had done up until that point. He told the *Nottingham Post* minutes after their performance: 'When we came off stage we were all completely shaking and trembling. The other gigs we've done were at Wembley and the O2, but this was literally the best crowd we've ever had. It was amazing. Everyone was bouncing and singing the words back. It was so good! I'm so buzzing! I'm grinning from ear to ear!'

Although only Jay has a real passion for dancing the other boys haven't been able to avoid the odd dance class or two. Their record company brought in Brian Friedman from *The X Factor* to help choreograph their performances in the bigger venues. They had to be able to move around on stage during the O2 and Wembley performances, otherwise their performance would have seemed rubbish compared to the other acts with whom they were sharing a stage. Audiences expected to see a bit of dancing – they didn't want to just see Jay, Max, Tom, Nathan and Siva stood rooted to the spot. Brian always made sure the boys tried really hard in their dance sessions, making them do press-ups as punishment when they didn't try hard enough.

Jay explained to the *Metro* how it worked: 'He did this big routine and then took out the bits we couldn't do. He made us look good doing the things we could do. He was clever with how he worked with us. If we could do backflips, we would, but we don't have the skills.'

Tom found performing in front of 70,000 people at Wembley at the Summertime Ball really emotional and one of his favourite performances to date. He told 95.8 Capital Radio shortly afterwards, 'It was the most incredible feeling of my life… when we first came off stage we were comparing who was shaking the most – it was me!'

The crowd loved them and Max couldn't believe it either because it was back in June 2010 when 'All Time Low' hadn't even been released. He had to say to himself during the performance, 'Don't dribble.' He didn't want to embarrass himself with so many people watching his every move: 'I was so excited and my mouth started watering and I was like "I'm definitely going to dribble." I don't think I dribbled.'

Before the event kicked off the boys were thinking that they didn't deserve to get to perform at Wembley because they didn't have a string of number one records under their belts, but they were just looking forward to going out and performing. Some performers have to wait years to get a gig at Wembley and it's the highlight of their careers. The Wanted boys achieved that goal straight away. Tom, Max, Siva, Nathan and Jay want to perform at Wembley again, and again and again.

The boys enjoyed having their own dressing room at Wembley and the free stuff they got was amazing. They each got an iPod touch which Max really appreciated because he'd never had one before. The night before Nathan had accidentally broken Max's laptop so he tried to make up for it by offering Max his iPod touch but Max wouldn't accept it. They also got giant bars of Dairy Milk, Guess watches, invitations to Champneys Health Resorts and a whole table of other great gifts. It was like Christmas. Later, when they were backstage they looked at all the dressing room doors and saw all the amazing artists who they would be sharing a stage with: Pixie Lott, Dizzee Rascal and Alexandra Burke... and many more. Max nipped to the toilet and thought he heard Alexandra Burke in the cubicle next to him – it made him so nervous he couldn't go. You can check out a cool backstage video of The Wanted at the Summertime Ball on YouTube.

'All Time Low' had only started getting played on the radio that week so the boys were surprised when about half of the crowd started singing along with them. They think the other half were trying to join in with the chorus.

Once their performance at Wembley finished they couldn't stop and reflect because they had to promote 'All Time Low' in as many places as possible. In the month and a half that followed they performed in front of approximately 300,000 people in total. That's a lot of performances.

> ### DID YOU KNOW?
> Even though they have done hundreds of performances, the boys still get really, really nervous before they go on stage. Sometimes they feel like they're going to have an unfortunate accident, but once the music comes on and they start singing they feel fine. Performing gives them such a buzz!

Photos

The boys love taking photos wherever they go. Tom is forever posting his photos to Twitter so that fans can see them. He takes photos of the band chilling out, on the move and random photos too. He's taken photos of some shoes with Tom lettering on the heel, a grid with TW on it and he took a photo of an old embarrassing photo of Max so he could share it with their fans.

Over the last year the boys have posed for thousands of photos with fans. It doesn't matter if they're having a bad day, if a fan wants a photo with them they'll always smile and give them a hug. They always put their fans first. Sometimes fans make lovely collages of the band with their fans and send them to the band via their fan mail address. Jay, Nathan, Max, Siva and Tom stick them on their walls at home or put them in a box so they can look

NATHAN AND JAY MEET FANS
AND SIGN AUTOGRAPHS.

at them whenever they want. In years to come they'll be able to look back at their photos and remember the good times and the funny times. It must be nice for their parents to look at the photos too, as they don't live with them anymore so miss out on so much.

Pixie Lott

Pixie Lott is a very gifted singer and Jay, Nathan, Max, Tom and Siva would love to get the chance to work with her one day. They think her first single 'Mama Do (Uh Oh, Uh Oh)' and her second single 'Boys and Girls' are really good and would love to collaborate with her.

Pixie is from London so knows all the best places to go and she has asked the boys to go on nights out with her a few times but they haven't yet. She did go back to their room with The Saturdays and Beverley Knight after a gig but the boys ended up standing them up because their management needed them to do something else instead. The girls haven't held it against them because they know how it feels to be so busy when you're promoting a single.

Max has a bit of a crush on Pixie and admitted to the *Mirror*: 'I chatted to Pixie Lott and she was very nice. But every time I tried to put in a cheeky word it was just palmed off with niceness. You have to love a trier.'

SARAH OLIVER

181

It would be nice if Pixie dated Max or one of the other boys because she is gorgeous, talented and has a lovely personality. She also knows how to handle fame and the paparazzi and wouldn't be intimated by the press attention.

Q is for...

Questions

The boys have done so many interviews in different countries now that they must be sick of hearing the same questions over and over again. Some interviewers are fans of the band or do a lot of research beforehand so they can ask more interesting questions that the band have never been asked before.

The boys think that their fans on Twitter, rather than trained journalists or presenters, ask the most interesting questions. Fans ask random things like 'What's your favourite colour Starburst.' They also help the boys out by answering the band's questions. When the clocks went back Tom was really

THE SPICE GIRLS:
GINGER, POSH, SCARY,
BABY AND SPORTY.

confused and tweeted 'What time is it' so fans replied and told him straight away. Other times fans just suggest things the band might want to do. Because Max is a huge footy fan they'll let him know when matches are on and what channel/time he needs to tune in to watch.

Fans have also asked The Wanted if they were the Spice Girls who would be who? They said Nathan would be Baby, Tom would be Geri, Jay would be Sporty, Max would be Scary which meant that Siva had to be Posh. It actually worked out well because Siva is quite posh. The boys loved this question because they thought they all fitted the names they picked. Tom and Max also admitted they both fancied Geri when the Spice Girls first came out (they probably still fancy her now as well).

During one Wanted Wednesday video a fan asked Tom to ask Max what was the funniest thing that had happened to him since being in the band. Rather than embarrass himself, Max spilled the beans on what happened when Jay met Frankie from The Saturdays after a gig. Siva was so glad that Max picked this story to tell. Max said that Jay started to cry because he'd had a lot to drink and was in an 'I love everyone' kind of mood. Jay didn't really want the story to go public but Max couldn't resist telling everyone.

In another video Max read out a fan's question to Nathan which was really good. It was 'If you had to kick out one member of the band and replace them with a celebrity who would it be?' Nathan wanted to say that he'd kick himself out and bring in Justin Bieber but Max, Jay, Tom and Siva wouldn't let that be his answer because they thought it was dodging the question. In the end Nathan said he'd get rid of Max and replace him with Shayne Ward, the former *X Factor* winner. Their manager Jayne was listening and said she'd never let that happen. She didn't see the point, she wanted him to pick someone more 'worthy.' Jay suggested they brought in Gary Barlow but then Jayne said they should bring in Robbie Williams and get rid of Tom. Poor Tom! By the end of their chat they said they'd get rid of Tom and Max, bring in Robbie and Gary, get rid of Siva and bring in Kumar, and replace Jay with his twin Tom. Then Nathan would be the only original member left.

Sometimes in interviews Jay, Max, Tom, Siva and Nathan decide to have a laugh and set each other tasks. During one interview with *Teen Today* they had a competition to see who could get the lowest on their chair without the interviewer noticing. Max and Jay were really good at it. The wriggled right down until only their heads were visible above the desk. In the same interview they also set themselves the challenge of throwing song lyrics into their answers. Siva was the first one with 'lose my mind', Jay was next with 'riding solo', then Siva mentioned 'get here'. It became a two member battle between Siva and Jay with Jay coming out on top. Jay managed to squeeze in 'man in the mirror', 'let's get physical' and 'so long, farewell' and 'I'm just a teenage dirtbag'. The interviewer didn't even notice.

Siva said during one Wanted Wednesday interview that if he was granted three wishes by a genie he would ask for: 1. World domination for The Wanted; 2. Unlimited supply of chocolate brownies; and 3. The ability to fly. Jay was asked in another Wanted Wednesday interview which member of the group he would pick to take with him if he was stuck on a desert island. He picked Max for two reasons: 1. He thinks Max would be able to handle himself and would be like British adventurer Bear Grylls; 2. Because he's a bigger build than the other three and if he died there would be more to eat. Yuck!

Another good question the boys have been asked in an interview was what super powers would they pick if they could pick anything. Tom stereotypically picked X-ray vision so he could see women naked, Siva said he wanted to be an Asian Superman and Max said he wanted the power to

control iTunes so 'All Time Low' could be at number
one for three years.

R is for...

Rihanna

Siva might have a long-term girlfriend called Nareesha but people haven't stopped linking him to 'Umbrella' superstar Rihanna since they got chatting at the Summertime Ball at Wembley in June 2010. That night they went with the rest of the boys to the club Mahiki. It's a Hawaiian theme club and lots of celebrities go there for nights out. Emma Watson, the Sugababes, Paris Hilton and Lindsay Lohan have all enjoyed nights at Mahiki with their friends.

Siva confessed to the *Metro*, 'It's true. I met her in a club. She is very nice and very tall. She gave me a dance, she's really nice – we did swap numbers.'

Siva and Rihanna have texted each other but there is no chance of them dating because they are both dating other people. Jay, Max, Tom and Nathan would love to have given their numbers to Rihanna but she only wanted Siva's.

When the first stories broke Siva wasn't bothered but as the months have gone on he must be sick of people talking about that night all the time. Now he hardly mentions it and keeps what they texted about a secret. The other boys enjoy talking about it though because they like winding Siva up.

Jay told the *Metro*, 'The night it happened Siva was told he wasn't allowed to say anything about it. From what I saw it looked pretty hot. She's 25 times out of our league.'

He likes saying that Siva took her to Greggs for a pasty the day after they met, and bought her a McFlurry from McDonald's. It didn't happen but it would be funny if it had.

S is for...

Scars

Tom was a bit accident prone when he was younger and he has four scars on his face. On one side of his forehead he has a scar from where he fell off a rocking horse, while on the other side of his forehead he has a scar from where he ran into a patio door thinking it was open. He has a football injury scar on his cheek and between his eyebrows he picked a chickenpox spot so has a scar there too.

He is so accident prone that when the boys decided to have a race around a park on manual go-karts he took a corner too hard, fell off and the seat fell off too. He was miles behind the rest by the time he fixed his go-kart. After they'd raced for a while they ended up crashing into each other for fun. Boys will be boys!

Tom told *Bliss*, 'If I get a scratch or a little dig, within two minutes I'll come up like a balloon. I got hit by a ball the other day and after five minutes I looked like Sylvester Stallone.'

Schools Tour

When they were first starting out, the boys' record company and management felt that doing a schools tour might be the best way to get their music to their potential audience. It meant a lot of performances and a lot of travel but Jay, Nathan, Tom, Max and Siva were more than up for it. They wanted to perform 'All Time Low' to an audience and see what they thought of it.

The first school they visited was Addington High School in Croydon. They didn't have far to go to get there but the boys were still very nervous. They didn't need to be – everyone who saw them perform loved it and the girls started picking who they liked the most straightaway. They gave out posters and other goodies so the kids had something to remember them by. Jay is very cheeky and after their performance he wrote on a desk in black pen and took a 'Senior Prefect' badge as a memento of the day. He couldn't help himself, and got told off by Jayne. Max was an absolute hero just for getting out of bed because he was so ill the morning of the performance. His throat was so sore he had porridge with honey in it and inhaled steam in the hope that it would help him get through the day as they had another performance at another school once they finished at Addington High School. He didn't want to let anyone down.

During their schools tour they did five schools a week and three performances in each school. They also went to some clubs too to let older people know what they were about. Doing more than 15 performances a week must have been very tiring but the boys never let it show. They always made sure that their fifteenth performance of the week was as good as their first. Max was surprised at how rowdy the kids were in some schools. Jay kept seeing 12 year olds holding up banners with their mobile numbers on which shocked him because it was something he'd never thought would happen, and they were so young too.

Jay talked about how the schools tour went to the *Metro*: 'At first they didn't care. They looked so bored, as if they'd prefer to be doing maths, but as things went on we got a really good reaction. Especially at girls' schools. They scream to the point where you think they're going to hurt themselves. It's invigorating but also a bit scary sometimes.'

Nathan was given the opportunity of playing at his

Max gets the crowd singing during a live performance.

old school, Ribston Hall High in Gloucester. This was a huge privilege because the other boys didn't get to perform at their old schools. Nathan found it a bit surreal because a few months earlier he'd still been a student there. He recognised so many students and teachers – it must have felt like he should have been sat with the other students watching instead of being on stage.

Nathan chatted to his friend Oscar about how he was feeling about performing at his school minutes before he was due on stage. The school had laid on a special buffet for the occasion. Nathan said, 'It's really weird… I'm not sure if I like it. It could go either really well… or really badly.' He was surprised at the reaction they got when they arrived because they didn't see him as Nathan, they saw him as a pop star. All the boys liked putting on an extra good show because it was Nathan's school and Jay had a bit of a crush on one of the teachers!

Nathan revealed to the *Daily Star*, 'We played a gig at my old school recently. It was crazy. I was one of only 11 boys in my year so it was all screaming ladies.' Siva added, 'Nathan's a modest bloke, so he wouldn't tell you that they were all chanting his name. He doesn't get embarrassed, though. He might be the youngest but he's the least nervous.'

After doing the first run of schools they had two

weeks off but when they came back they were surprised when people started singing 'All Time Low' back to them. Before then the school kids had just watched in silence. The kids that knew the lyrics must have checked out the boys on YouTube and read what other kids had said about them online. Before long, fan groups were being set up on Facebook.

Siva

Siva Kaneswaran was born and raised in Dublin, Ireland. His name means pure. He is the joint tallest member of The Wanted as he is 6'1" just like Jay but he looks taller sometimes because he is slighter than Jay. He might describe himself as being tall, dark and handsome but he does have the odd ginger hair. His mum has ginger hair so it's in his genes. He is half Sri-Lankan and half Irish.

As well as fans having their favourite members of The Wanted, journalists and presenters can have their favourites too. A writer from the website EQ wrote in one article, 'Siva is the most polite and considerate member of The Wanted. I sat next to him during the interview and he was the first one to offer up a chair and make you feel comfortable. Every time you looked over at him, he would just flash his million dollar smile to let you know all was cool. You don't know how

many times I've done interviews and the pop star in question has a "greater than thou" attitude. Not with Siva though, he's a total gent and a total star.'

Moving in with the boys was probably the easiest for Siva and Max. Max had shared a house with the members of Avenue and Siva has seven brothers and sisters so he was used to sharing with a lot of people. He was used to having to queue to use the bathroom or having to compromise over what to have for dinner. Having so many brothers and sisters has helped Siva become the confident young man he is today. His family have always supported his wish to be a singer and are behind him every step of the way.

Like Jay, who has a twin called Tom, Siva has a twin called Kumar. The name Kumar means Prince. It is very unusual for a boy band to have a member that is a twin, let alone a band to have two members who are twins. Siva and his twin Kumar are identical and only their family and closest friends can tell the difference. It would be funny if Siva and Kumar switched places on April Fool's Day and Kumar went around with Jay, Max, Tom and Nathan for the day.

Growing up, Siva and Kumar might have been the youngest members of their family but they weren't mollycoddled. They had to do chores just like anyone else. Siva told *OK!* magazine they were 'like the Cinderellas of the family, always doing the work!'

Gail is the oldest of the Kaneswaran children, followed by Hazel, David, Daniel, Kelly, Trevor, Kumar and Siva. Only Kelly out of all eight of the Kaneswaran children is taking a non musical/modelling route – she is currently a student.

Kumar auditioned for the band with Siva and another of their brothers did too. Kumar wasn't too upset when he didn't get in because he enjoys modelling but the other brother was gutted. Kumar is at college and is still doing modelling. In the future he might go to university because he wants to get an education. Siva hasn't got the time to study because he's so busy with the band but he might decide to get a degree one day.

Siva grew up in the working class Blanchardstown area of Dublin. At Christmas the Kaneswaran kids would all crowd around in their living room and sing together; they loved performing as a group. You would struggle to find a closer family. Siva's mum likes nothing better than having her kids around her dinner table on a Sunday tucking into a roast dinner. This can be tricky nowadays because her kids don't all live in Ireland any more but they probably make a special effort when Siva comes home to visit. They are so proud of him.

Siva's family are famous in Ireland and have been for a number of years. They are good looking and super talented – with most of Siva's brothers and sisters having an interest in singing, modelling or both!

The first member of the Kaneswaran family to be famous was Siva's brother David. He was in an Irish boy band called ZOO. They were huge in Ireland and supported Westlife and Brian McFadden on tour. They parted ways in October 2006 and David formed a songwriting and production company with his former band mate Eric. He now writes songs with their brother Daniel. They have called their writing partnership DKMY. He is a model too.

Daniel is another talented songwriter and has been writing great songs since he was 15. If you want to check out his music, visit www.myspace.com/dkmy08.

Their sister Hazel was in a popular Irish girl band called Dove before auditioning for *Popstars: The Rivals* in 2002. She got through to the last 10 but was thrown off for being 10 days too old. Kimberley Walsh replaced her and ended up winning a place in Girls Aloud. Hazel was heavily pregnant at the time and many people thought that was the real reason she was kicked off. She was more relieved than anything because she was due to give birth a week after she was told she was going home. She went on to be a judge on the Irish equivalent of *The X Factor*, called *You're a Star* (her sister later went on to be in the celebrity version). She had a successful solo career and three Top 10 singles. Nowadays she writes music for other artists and Louis Walsh thinks she's amazing. He asked her for some songs for Jedward and she sent him two he could use.

On her official website biography it talks about her dad: 'Her dad was one of the first coloured people in the neighbourhood and, as the local window-cleaner in a paddy cap, proved a massively popular local figure. He loved soul music and passed that love onto his daughter. Hazel's dad died suddenly at the age of 44, and as Hazel is the second oldest in a family of eight, she had to help her mother out by looking after her six younger brothers.'

Poor Siva and Kumar were only six at the time so it must have been hard for them to understand that they wouldn't be seeing their dad again. He had only gone to get a takeaway when he had his heart attack.

Siva's sister Gail is one of Ireland's top models and socialites. She took part in the Irish TV series *Charity You're a Star* in 2006. Ten celebrities took part and in each episode the celebrity who received the least votes was voted off. Gail's chosen charity was Our Lady's Children's Hospital in Crumlin. The former Liverpool and Republic of Ireland footballer John Aldridge won the series. She is quite a bit older than Siva; she's in her thirties and she has two children.

Siva's brother Trevor is a songwriter and he has written songs with Siva in the past. In 2008 he appeared

on *The X Factor* and made it to the boot camp stage. Gail told Herald.ie at the time, 'We used to slag him saying he learned to sing before he could talk as he has been at it since he was three years old when he went in for this local talent show and won it. It's all he has ever wanted to do. He really wants to make it big, and who wouldn't want to be in a programme like *The X Factor*? Ever since Hazel was in Popstars, our whole family has been mad about the show and we would always watch it in our house every Saturday.'

If you want to learn more about Trevor, head over to his MySpace page: www.myspace.com/trevorkaneswara. In his biography he says he was in a band with three of his brothers for a while but he doesn't say which brothers. No one else in the family has mentioned this band in interviews before but it would be cool if they reformed. They are all so gorgeous!

Siva's mum Lily is so proud of her children and all they have achieved. The Kaneswarans are proof that you can come from a rough area but still make something of yourself. There were tough times in the past when her children were small that Lily had to make food stretch because she had so many mouths to feed but it made them stronger as a family. Lily always made her children smile, as Siva revealed to the *Daily Star*: 'My mum used to encourage us all to express ourselves. She was always taking us to karaoke. I think my confidence

SIVA AND MAX MEET
THEIR ADORING FANS.

comes from being part of such a big family. We're all very supportive of each other.'

THREE FASCINATING FACTS ABOUT SIVA

• He has silk sheets on his bed (which the other boys find highly amusing).

• He likes sitting on his own watching movies.

• He loves candles and has loads of them in his room – he's very romantic and doesn't care that the other lads think it's a bit girly!

Stress

People think that being a boy band must be an easy job but it really isn't. Tom, Max, Siva, Jay and Nathan are under immense stress sometimes and they have had to learn how to channel it. They feel under pressure to make each new single bigger and better than the one before – which is a tough challenge because all of The Wanted's songs are so good.

When Tom is feeling stressed he chills out by playing his guitar and singing quietly to himself. Nathan likes to sit at a piano and try to make up his own songs. All the boys know they can pick up the phone at any time of the day or night and call their manager Jayne or their parents for help and advice.

The boys know that stress is something that comes along with being a pop star. They told Orange: 'We all know it's quite a ruthless industry we've chosen to be in. I think if you're going to find that difficult then it's not the career for you. It's just very different because it changes so quickly.'

T is for...

Take That

From day one, The Wanted have always been asked how they feel about Take That and if they want to be the new Take That. Tom in particular is a huge Take That fan.

He told 4Music, 'I love the fact that Take That have come back. I was so surprised when 'Patience' came out. I've got massive respect for Gary Barlow in particular. To invent a new sound for them was incredible.'

If each member of The Wanted had to pick one member of Take That that they are most similar to then Tom would be Mark, Jay would be Howard because he dances, Nathan would be Gary because he plays the

piano, Siva would be Jason because he was a model and Max would be Robbie. Max was happy being 'Robbie', he told 4Music: 'I'm just gonna go and chill with Guy Chambers.'

Although the boys want to do big tours on their own they would jump at the opportunity to support Take That on tour. They would learn so much from Gary, Mark, Jason, Howard and Robbie. They know exactly what The Wanted are going through because many years ago they were the new kids on the block. They might also help them deal with any clashes that may occur in the future and prevent things escalating. Right now there are no issues because Siva, Max, Tom, Nathan and Jay get on so well but there might be the odd disagreement in the future.

The Wanted told Orange that they'd like to be as successful as Take That, 'and for our shows to be in the same league as them – they're amazing! But as for modelling ourselves on anyone we'd just like to be ourselves. It's a bit weird cause we don't see ourselves as famous – we're just five lads that are enjoying ourselves. It's odd when paps are chasing us on motorbikes or when girls cry when they meet us… it's like "we're okay, we don't bite!"'

Tattoos

When they're travelling in their van they like to draw tattoos on each other with Sharpies felt tip pens. Jay drew a full armful of tattoos on Max's arm on their way to Glasgow. He drew a skull and crossbones, a naked woman, a sun and vines all the way up his arm. It looked so good – like a proper tattoo. Jay is so good at drawing. It's a good job Max didn't get ink poisoning. Max loves tattoos and thinks that girls with tattoos are hot.

They also drew a tribal design on Siva's face on the same day which must have made people stare when he got out of their van and had to go wash it off.

Some fans get Max, Tom, Jay, Nathan and Siva to sign their boobs. In the future some of these fans might visit tattoo parlours and ask for the tattoo artist to turn the autographs into tattoos. The boys would be so surprised to see fans with their signatures tattooed to their boobs or arms. Tom in particular would be shocked because he changes his signature all the time so it would probably have changed since the last he saw the fans. He would have to keep that to himself otherwise the girls could get really mad or upset.

Nathan has said in the past that he thinks all the members of the group will end up getting The Wanted tattooed on their bums one day. They all love being in the group so much and never want to have to separate.

The Saturdays

The boys are really close to the girl band The Saturdays. They have known them for almost as long as they have known each other because Jayne Collins put The Saturdays together and they have supported them on tour too. Both bands are made up of British and Irish members who are gorgeous and super talented singers.

The Saturdays have been going for a lot longer than The Wanted, as they were put together in 2007, but they are still waiting for their first number one. The boys think that Frankie Sandford, Rochelle Wiseman, Una Healy, Mollie King and Vanessa White are awesome girls and wish them every success.

The girls released their first album back in 2008. *Chasing Lights* gave them four top 10 singles: 'If This Is Love' reached number eight in the charts, 'Up' reached number five, 'Issues' reached number four and 'Just Can't Get Enough' came in at number two. They did release a fifth song from the album but it failed to make the top 10 or even the top 20. 'Work' charted at a disappointing 22 in the charts. The girls didn't write any of the tracks on this album.

The girls started out supporting Girls Aloud on tour but got to headline their own tour in June 2009. It was called 'The Work Tour' and as they toured they started working on their second album *Wordshaker*. When the album was released in October 2009 it made number nine in the albums chart. Their single 'Forever is Over' reached number two in the charts and their second single from the album, 'Ego', made it to number nine. The album is no longer available for download but some of the tracks are featured on the band's mini-album *Headlines* which was released in August 2010. Their track 'Missing You' from Headlines was tipped to ·

come in at number one in the charts when it was released on 5 August 2010 but it only managed to reach number three. It had been leading in the midweek figures but was beaten by 'Club Can't Handle Me' by Flo Rida and 'Love the Way You Lie' by Eminem and Rihanna.

On 28 August 2010, it was reported that JLS would like to do a duet with The Saturdays. Rochelle is dating Marvin from JLS so it wasn't a big shock for fans of either band. Many fans of The Wanted will be gutted if The Saturdays record a track with JLS because they would like the girls to do something with The Wanted instead.

Frankie, Rochelle, Una, Mollie and Vanessa were given their own reality TV show in August 2010 called *The Saturdays: 24/7*. It was shown over four weeks on ITV2. It's only a matter of time before Siva, Jay, Tom, Max and Nathan are offered their own reality TV show. An ideal time for any documentary style reality TV show to be filmed would be during the boys' first tour. Fans would love to watch them behind the scenes as they rehearse, perform and relax.

The boys really like The Saturdays but they love Girls Aloud too. They think The Saturdays are fit… and they feel the same way about Girls Aloud (especially Cheryl). They feel a lot of love for girl bands!

The papers are always linking members of The

Wanted with members of The Saturdays. The boys don't mind that much because the girls are so attractive. In an ideal world Tom would probably like it if they all hooked up with a member of The Saturdays so they could go on big dates together. There might be five lads and five girls but Siva is dating someone and a few members of The Saturdays are in serious relationships too.

Jay told the *News of the World*, 'They're all gorgeous. Because we have the same management, we've been to quite a few of their gigs and we speak to them quite a lot, especially Frankie and Rochelle – they're really lovely and so friendly.

'There's five of them and five of us, so the lads have obviously had the conversation about who would go with whom! Max has quite a big crush on Frankie... but I think she might have a boyfriend!'

The press seem to think differently to Jay and reckon that Vanessa is the Saturday Max fancies the most. He disagrees with both Jay and the press as he says Mollie is his favourite. When the boys discuss their favourite member of The Saturdays they can be prone to changing their minds it seems. At the moment Jay likes Vanessa, Siva likes Una (purely as a mate though!), Tom likes Frankie and Nathan likes Rochelle. Max has said in the past that he likes Rochelle, but that he's scared of Marvin.

The boys love winding each other up whenever they can and during one interview with ASOS they decided to pick on Nathan. Jay told the website, 'Nathan's the world's biggest Saturdays fan, he's got the coloured tights and he's in love with Rochelle.' Tom added, 'He'll take on Marvin. Nathan's a beast of a man.'

The *Metro* asked Jay in an interview whether The Saturdays had given the band any advice about the music business. He replied, 'No, we just talk about stuff that you'd talk to mates at uni about. Not work. We've taught them how to play football but they haven't taught us anything.'

The boys loved teaching the girls how to play football. They though Vanessa was really good fun and was probably the best at football because she could kick the ball a good distance. Frankie was surprisingly bad and couldn't play very well at all. She might need a few more lessons from the boys to get up to Vanessa's standard.

The boys might have said in interviews how much they like The Saturdays but the girls rarely mention the boys when they get interviewed. When the *Daily Star* talked to Mollie about boy bands she said, 'As far as I'm concerned, girls are dominating and will for a long time.

'The guys have still got a long way to go. I'm a very girl power person and love Katy Perry and Girls

Aloud. When Girls Aloud return to the scene – and that will hopefully be soon – then there'll be absolutely no competition.'

We will just have to wait and see because at the moment boy bands do seem to be leading the way with girl bands trailing behind – whatever Mollie says!

Tom

Tom was born Thomas Parker on 4 August 1988. He is the oldest member of The Wanted by a month (Max was born next, on 6 September, but would have been in the year below if they had gone to the same school).

Tom is from Bolton which is a town in Greater Manchester. He isn't the first famous person to come from Bolton – boxer Amir Khan, comedian Peter Kay and presenter Vernon Kay all come from the town. Tom supports his local football team Bolton Wanderers.

Tom is 5'10" so is the middle member of The Wanted in terms of height. He is one of the band's best singers even though he didn't have any singing lessons before joining the band. Tom told Industry Music, 'People like Stereophonics and Liam Gallagher had a big influence on me. I've got a really throaty, rock voice, I'm glad I never had any singing lessons, they try to teach you a certain way. I just kinda taught myself.'

Tom's family had no idea that he was going to be a

singer when he was growing up because he wasn't into performing on stage or singing in front of an audience like Nathan was. He only decided that music was something he wanted to do when he was sixteen and his brother encouraged him to pick up a guitar. Siva was exactly the same.

Once he decided music was what he wanted to do he set about joining a band. Tom was in a Take That tribute band for a while, playing Mark Owen even though he doesn't look anything like him. He had to have his hair long so he could style it to be like Mark's. Take That 2 were the one of the best tribute bands in the country. They formed as soon as the real Take That made their comeback album and they were soon booked for every Thursday, Friday and Saturday night for a year. They became so popular that they held auditions for another Take That tribute band so they could share their gigs. Their official MySpace page biography states: 'Take That 2 were chosen to appear at the O2 Arena on the same day as the real Take That! An accolade indeed! Furthermore they are also helping to promote the "Autograph" clothing range across the UK for Marks & Spencer. They have also just recently finished a two week stint performing at the No.7 Make-up Range Awards 2008 for Boots! If professionalism, quality, talent & a highly polished theatrical show is what you're looking for, then the only choice in the UK has to be

TAKE THAT 2. Not only are all 4 lads from the same area as the real TAKE THAT boys, our "Gary Barlow" possibly came from the same womb as the real Mr Barlow! The voice, look & mannerisms are quite simply outstanding! With no expense spared, and no corners cut, this really is the most professional tribute show package available today! You really do have to witness the phenomenon that is TAKE THAT 2! No other show pulls in the crowds or gets re-booked as fast as TAKE THAT 2!'

Tom loved being in Take That 2 and his former bandmates Danny Maines (Gary), Tom Patrick (Howard) and Daniel Claxton (Jason) enjoyed every minute of working with Tom. The management company who put Take That 2 together did a video for Tom on their website to congratulate their original Mark Owen on getting to number one with 'All Time Low'. They wrote, 'You're honest, genuine and deserve it.'

Tom might have loved being in Take That 2 but nothing compares with being in The Wanted. He might have toured all over as Mark Owen but nothing beats being able to sing as Tom Parker and having the opportunity to work with some of the best songwriters in the country.

Tom and Max are the loudest members of the band and love a good party. They spend the most time together and Tom admits, 'We'll pretty much leather it at any party going. But all the lads know how to have a laugh – maybe Nath's not reached that crazy part of his life yet, but we'll bring it out in him soon enough!'

They can't party all the time and work really hard in the studio when they are recording new songs or when they're doing interviews or performances. They know that being in the band is a privilege and won't let anything mess it up.

When 'All Time Low' got to number one they partied for a month because they were so happy. They haven't let the success go to their heads though – they know it is all down to their fans going out and buying the single.

Tom confided in his local paper, the *Bolton News*: 'I can't quite believe that a year ago I was sat in Bolton, doing nothing, dreaming about being in the music industry and with thanks to a certain lady called Jayne Collins, and obviously my mum and dad… and last but not least the fans for going out buying it and getting it to number one, they've made it all possible!'

THREE FASCINATING FACTS ABOUT TOM

- Tom went to the same school as Danny Jones from McFly.

- Tom likes to be tanned all the time. Once when he was feeling pale he tweeted: 'I am the palest person ever... Might get @Jaynecollinsmac to cover me in fake tan from head to toe... Literally!!!'

- Tom has made his dad famous. Nigel Parker now has his own Facebook fan page and answers fans' questions on there. Just go to Facebook and search for 'Tom's Dad (The Wanted)'. He also gets recognised when he's out and about and people have asked for his autograph.

Touring

Ever since they were first put together Jay, Siva, Tom, Nathan and Max have wanted to do their own arena tour but they knew they would have to do a lot of work to earn the right to do one. Tours cost so much money and their management would have to be confident that they would be a sell out before they could give them the thumbs up.

When 'All Time Low' reached number one, the

MAX AND TOM TAKE A WALK WHILST PROMOTING 'ALL TIME LOW'.

boys knew that they could do a tour but they also realised that the time was not quite right. They thought February/March 2011 would be the ideal time because their album would have been out for four months by then. They needed the album to come out first because they couldn't tour with only one song having been in the charts – otherwise fans wouldn't know what to expect and they wouldn't be able to sing along either.

Girls are currently banned from The Wanted tour van unless they are Jayne or from the record company but the boys want this rule changing. They spend so much time on the road that it would be easier if Siva's girlfriend could travel with them sometimes or if they found a girl they liked they could invite her onboard to meet the rest of the guys.

Choreographer Brian Friedman has already helped the boys work on routines for their performances at the O2 and Wembley but choreographing an arena tour is a much bigger job. Each song needs its own theme, dancers and set. They need to be able to go from one song to another, and get changed into different outfits in a matter of seconds. They also need to have a high level of fitness to be able to do this every night for weeks on end.

Take That set the standard in 2009 with their Circus Live tour. It cost £10 million and they had over 50 dancers, acrobats and circus performers. They rode a 30ft mechanical elephant and put on an amazing show. The Wanted will have to think big to be able to beat that!

The boys wouldn't want to disappoint fans so they'll be singing live and playing instruments too. Siva, Tom, and Max want to show off their guitar playing skills and Nathan can play the piano for one or two of their slower numbers.

U is for...

Underwear

When boy bands perform on stage girls are known to throw their underwear at them – sometimes with their mobile numbers written on them. This isn't something new.

The Wanted boys also get underwear sent to their fan mail address or handed to them by fans as presents. One fan bought Jay some lovely bright boxers for his birthday but Max got to them first and wore them before Jay had chance to. Jay didn't mind though; the lads swap clothes all the time. If they see a nice top hanging around their house they just wear it, regardless of who it belongs to. Having a stylist who picks out the clothes they wear to interviews or to perform in means that the boys aren't very possessive about clothes. It shows how comfortable they are with each other if they'll wear each other's underwear!

Sometimes the band give out their underwear as prizes. The boys ran a competition to win something from their house and picked Laura Hodgkinson to win the prize – a pair of Tom's boxers. She cried tears of happiness when she found out she'd won and kept checking the post every day until they arrived two weeks later.

She tweeted: @TomTheWanted 'guess what I got through the post on Wednesday!! Your boxers!! Thankyou so much for signing them, you actually don't understand how happy you have made me, I think I'm the luckiest girl in this world you know!!!!! :) I'm BUZZING! Thankyouu! Can you please please follow me?!?!?! Love you so much <3 xxxx'

They were Next boxers and Tom wrote 'To Laura, Hope you like the boxers and they don't smell too much. Lots of love Tom x'

Laura is a huge fan of The Wanted and has had a tweet from every member of the band apart from Max – but she's working on getting one from him too, because she wants the full set!

V is for...

Vanity

When it comes to vanity it's hard to say who is the most vain member of the band. Tom, Siva, and Nathan spend the longest time in front of the mirror and Max says it's hard to pick out who's the worst out of the three of them. Jay isn't bothered really. He can just roll out of bed in the morning and he's ready to go. If they had to say who's the most confident looking in the mirror they would pick Siva, even though he strongly disagrees. He knows he's good looking but he still has ugly days like anyone else. Tom thinks he is the least confident about the way he looks.

DID YOU KNOW?

Tom uses hairspray before big TV interviews to make sure that his hair looks just right. For one photo shoot his fringe was looking too thin so they made him wear hair extensions!

Voting

Nathan found it really frustrating that he couldn't vote in the 2010 General Election because he was one year too young at 17. He thinks it's ridiculous that you can drive a car when you're seventeen but you can't vote. He's joined Anastasia Kyriacou's 'Where's Our Vote' campaign to try and get the law changed so that people aged 16+ can vote. Jay also feels strongly about the subject even though he hasn't voted yet and the rest of The Wanted boys are backing Anastasia too.

Anastasia spoke to the Wanted lads in the flesh at The Transformation Trust's free gig event at the O2 on 13 July 2010 and she had another chat to Nathan via Twitter on 22 July:

@WheresOurVote 'How did you feel about being unable to vote on election day?'

@NathanTheWanted 'I felt baaaddd! I felt excluded from the situation even though people my age had been given a false belief that we were

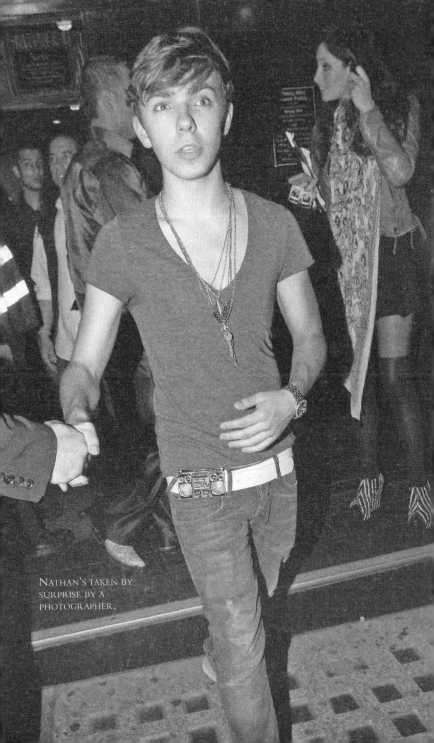

NATHAN'S TAKEN BY
SURPRISE BY A
PHOTOGRAPHER.

important to society, almost as if they didn't care about our opinion!'

@WheresOurVote 'TELL ME ABOUT IT – It's as if our voices are irrelevant! Hmm, so would you have voted if you had the chance?'

@NathanTheWanted 'Exactly! And they go on about us havin "responsibilities" at our age! And yes! I defo would have voted! As would quite a few people I know! But it's crazy coz they think that we would mis-use our vote and vote for the "wrong party" because we don't know enough about life!!'

@WheresOurVote 'I KNOW – whilst we're given no right to vote, they have no right to make assumptions! Feelings on new government?'

@NathanTheWanted 'I know! Talk about 1 rule 4 1 n 1 4 the other! I'm gonna be interested on the decisions they're gonna hav to make, after labour was in gov 4 13yrs, the cons r gonna hav 2 make changes durin these times and it will be nice to hav a different way of runnin the country!'

If you want to join the Wanted boys and Anastasia go to YouTube and search for 'Where's Our Vote'.

W is for...

Wanted Wednesday

Every fan of The Wanted needs to get involved with Wanted Wednesday on Twitter and Facebook. The band explained what it's all about on their YouTube channel: 'It's a chance for you to get closer to the band. You get to tell the world what you want on Twitter and Facebook. Upload a picture of what you want on Twitter and Facebook and make sure to tell all your friends about Wanted Wednesday. Upload a video on Wednesday and you could be 'fan of the week'. Tag all your tweets with #wantedwednesday and tag the wanted Facebook fan page in your status updates. It's the next best thing after Follow Friday, better than that even. More fun, more Wanted and its definitely more Wednesday. Watch out for a special Wanted Wednesday video every week.'

Since fans started to do tweets with #wantedwednesday at the front it has become a worldwide trending topic on Twitter and fans from so many different countries have been taking part. This will really help the band become famous all around the world and might even result in a world tour one day. That would be awesome!

The Wanted Wednesday videos are the best as each week the band come up with a different opening before they all start shouting 'It's Wanted Wednesday' and run around like nutters. It's a bit like the opening to *The Simpsons* – you never know what to expect. The best opening so far was when Jay shows the camera around his room as he's on his own and the rest of the band jump out of the built in wardrobes and hang out of the cupboards at the top. They've also pretended to be dogs running around a park – goodness knows what people in the park thought of five lads on all fours barking and sniffing each other.

On Wednesdays the band let their fans know what they want. On Wednesday 30 June Siva wanted cola botttles, Tom wanted bananas, Max wanted some tracksuit shorts and Nathan wanted a pair of jeans and everyone to pre-order 'All Time Low'. On Wednesday

19 May, Tom wanted a pretzel, Siva wanted Crunchy Nut Cornflakes, Nathan wanted a safe flight home and Max wanted 'a head massage by a Chinese therapist.'

On Wednesdays they also send out an email newsletter to fans who have opted in to receive them on their official website. In it they fill everyone in on what they've been doing that week and show exclusive pictures that can't be seen anywhere else. If you haven't registered yet, head over to www.thewantedmusic.com.

X is for...

X Factor

The X Factor is Max's favourite show. He loves seeing the massive changes singers go through on the show, and he understands exactly how they are feeling when they get told their journey has come to an end because of what he experienced with Avenue when they appeared on the show. Max is a massive Simon Cowell fan. When he was on the show back when he was 16 he was immensely flattered when Simon said he was like Robbie Williams.

In August 2010 the boys asked their fans to retweet RT @Sy_Cowell: 'ReTweet if you would like The Wanted to appear on The X Factor.' All the boys would

X-Factor judge, Simon Cowell.

love the opportunity to perform on one of the *X Factor* results shows or duet with one of the finalists. Jay has even said he would shave his head if they did. Jay would look so weird bald so fans are hoping that he won't go through with it even if Simon Cowell gives them the thumbs up.

It's well known that Max was on *The X Factor* but Tom actually auditioned for the show too. He only got through to the first round and he wasn't picked to be on TV – which is a good thing now, but at the time he must have been gutted. Jay has admitted that he might have tried it himself if he hadn't got in The Wanted because he'd been to so many auditions and got nowhere.

Y is for...

YouTube

You really need to check out the boys' channel on YouTube because they've got so many great behind the scenes interviews on there.

When they first started out they had a competition running on their official Facebook page for a fan to pick a track they should cover. They had so many good entries that they couldn't decide which to pick so ended up picking out of a hat. They filmed themselves recording the winning song, 'Fight For This Love' (suggested by Annabelle) and posted it on YouTube. In it Tom plays the guitar and they all sing along. Tom does so well and it's great that he put the time in to learn it,

THE BOYS AFTER A
LIVE PERFORMANCE OF
'ALL TIME LOW'.

as it would have been easier for him if they sang without any musical accompaniment. It is a great version of the song and many people would say it's better than the original. They filmed the video in their house and you can see a *Con Air* movie poster and a *Rocky* poster on the wall because it was shot in Max's room. From the window behind Jay you can see the reflection of the TV – they were watching a footy match at the same time!

The song was such a hit that the record company decided to include it as the B side for 'All Time Low'.

Each week The Wanted pick a Fan of the Week from videos posted on YouTube. You have to think of a creative way to express how much you like the band. Some people make their own versions of the 'All Time Low' video, some people do photo collages set to music and other people take songs and change the lyrics so they are singing about Jay, Siva, Max, Nathan and Tom. You can do whatever you want to do and once you've posted it up The Wanted and other fans will look at it and give you great comments. Even if you don't win Fan of the Week it is still an amazing feeling to know that the boys have watched your video.

Z is for...

Zoo

When Siva's brother David was in the band Zoo with Barry Cosgrove, Eric McCarthy, Michael Sammon and Greg Ryan, Siva was so proud and happy for his big brother. It's a shame that Zoo aren't still going because it would have been nice to see both bands playing at the same gig. David is right behind Siva and wants The Wanted to be really successful.

Jay is a big fan of zoos (the ones with animals not the band) and likes going to see the lizards and other reptiles. He can't really go anymore because he would be swamped by lots of fans.

Some interviewers have asked the boys silly questions

relating to zoos in the past. MTV asked each member of The Wanted what was the biggest animal they could kill with their bare hands. Tom answered lion, Jay answered cow, Siva answered giraffe, Nathan answered elephant and Max answered killer whale. When the boys questioned how Max could kill a killer whale he said he would drain the pool out at Aqua Land. It might have been a rubbish question but Max gave a great answer.